D0344331

DATE DUE

DEMCO 38-297

THE PERSIAN GULF
AND
AMERICAN POLICY

THE PERSIAN GULF
AND
AMERICAN POLICY

Emile A. Nakhleh

PRAEGER

PRAEGER SPECIAL STUDIES • PRAEGER SCIENTIFIC

327.09536
N143p

Library of Congress Cataloging in Publication Data

Nakhleh, Emile A., 1938–
   The Persian Gulf and American Policy.

   Bibliography: p.
   Includes index.
   1. Persian Gulf Region—Politics and government.
2. Persian Gulf Region—Foreign relations—United
States. 3. United States—Foreign relations—Persian
Gulf Region. I. Title.
DS326.N24   1982   327'0953'6   82-13125
ISBN 0-03-060594-6

Published in 1982 by Praeger Publishers
CBS Educational and Professional Publishing
A Division of CBS Inc.
521 Fifth Avenue, New York, New York 10175 U.S.A.

© 1982 by Praeger Publishers

All rights reserved

456789 052 98765432
Printed in the United States of America

PREFACE

This book is one of many studies on the Persian Gulf and on the United States' recent relations with that part of the world. The basic assumption of the author is that the United States as a superpower has worldwide interests and therefore cannot be oblivious to developments in any area where U.S. interests are involved. Two other assumptions should be mentioned: the Persian Gulf/Arabian Peninsula region is an area in which the United States has vital interests; and a commonality of interest between the United States and gulf countries exists, although this is marred by serious disagreements such as the Palestinian conflict.

Such concepts as security, stability, cooperation, and development from a gulf perspective will be examined. The central questions throughout the book are how gulf governments and peoples define these concepts and how do they view their future as viable sovereign states in a world of superpower rivalry and continued regional conflicts? Of course, underlying these questions is the hypothesis that for U.S. interests to be served and protected, U.S. policy makers must become aware of regional perceptions, interests, and concerns and understand how internal forces have an impact on stability and instability in the region.

This volume results from many years of research on and visits to the Arab countries of the gulf, starting with a yearlong residence in Bahrain (1972-73) as a Fulbright senior research fellow. Since then, I have visited the region at least once a year to collect research data. Over the years, I have interviewed gulf rulers, university professors and students, senior civil servants, labor leaders, journalists, literati, heads of organizations, businessmen, security officials, ambassadors, diplomats, and even military leaders and naval officials (both indigenous and foreign).

On the U.S. side I have spoken to numerous officials involved in Washington's Persian Gulf policy making both at the Department of State and the Department of Defense. Particularly useful were my conversations with the U.S. commanders of the U.S. Middle East Force in the gulf, homeported in Bahrain. Furthermore, I have followed the gulf press closely, and although a strong tradition of free press is still lacking in many gulf states, some widely read newspapers such as al-Khaleej (Dubai) and al-Qabas (Kuwait) have provided a form for indigenous thought on important regional issues. Unfortunately for many English-speaking readers, the bulk of contemporary writings in gulf publications are in Arabic. Much material was translated by the author for the writing of this book.

In transliterating Arabic names, an attempt has been made to follow the most common form, both here and in the gulf. For example, in this book the name of the leader of Bahrain is Shaikh 'Isa bin Sulman al-Khalifa, even though "shaikh" and "sulman" according to the Library of Congress transliteration system are "shaykh" and "salman." This is also the case with "Bahrain" (as used here) and "Bahrayn" and with "Hussein" (as used here) and "Husayn." Furthermore, "amir" is used in this book as a title meaning "ruler," such as "the amir of Bahrain . . ." or "Shaikh 'Isa bin Sulman al-Khalifa is the amir of Bahrain." "Prince" is used to describe members of the Saudi royal family such as "Prince Fahd." Examples are "Crown Prince Fahd" or "Crown Prince Hassan." In the smaller amirates, "heir apparent" is used instead of "crown prince." An amirate is of course the domain of the amir, and in this case the term refers to the amirates of the United Arab Emirates. The others, although generically amirates, are described as states, such as the state of Bahrain, or the state of Qatar. Oman, however, is known as the sultanate of Oman, and its ruler is known as the sultan of Oman.

One final point about names should be mentioned. The use of the term "Persian Gulf" merely reflects common usage in the West; no ideological message is intended whatsoever. Of course if the book were translated into Arabic, and since the Arab states of the gulf used "Arabian" instead of "Persian," the author would not object to having the translated title read The Arabian Gulf and American Policy.

ACKNOWLEDGMENTS

In the course of research for this book, I have called on many people for ideas, opinions, and data. Many others were also involved in making the necessary arrangements for my numerous visits to gulf countries and for the many interviews conducted with political leaders and other opinion makers. Simply stated, I could not have done research in the gulf without the conscious support of many people. To all of them, I offer my sincere thanks.

Of course, as a professor and a department chairman, I could not have travelled as much as was necessary for this research without the support of the administration of Mount Saint Mary's College. I am therefore grateful to the president of the college, Dr. Robert J. Wickenheiser, and to the dean of the college, Dr. John W. Campbell, for their encouragement.

In the gulf, I would like to mention a few people for their very special help and friendship over the years: Tareq al-Moayyad, Jasim Murad, 'Ali Murad, Jasim Fakhru, 'Ali al-Amin, Hasan Fakhru, Muhammad Jasim al-Shirawi, Ahmad Kamal, Salman Taqi, Dr. Rod Wannebo, Muhammad Kamal al-Shahabi, Hisham al-Shahabi, Ibrahim Bashmi, Dr. Muhammad al-Khozai, Nabil Hammar, Dr. Hamad Slayti, Isa al Kuwari, Qusay al-'Abadlah, Muhammad Amin al-Ghayyath, and Tiryam Tiryam.

On the home and office fronts, I extend my most sincere thanks to my wife for her diligent, meticulous, and professional editing of this manuscript and of course for her endless patience, particularly during the last few months of writing. My secretary, June Myrick, not only supported me during this entire project, but also typed the manuscript, proofread it, and prepared it for the publisher. I simply could not have done it without her, and I am very grateful.

Finally, I want to thank Betsy Brown, editor at Praeger, for her accommodating understanding whenever I found it necessary to request an extension. In her wisdom, she has become familiar with and tolerant of the endemic disease of academics—overscheduling and overcommitment!

Emile A. Nakhleh

CONTENTS

LIST OF TABLES

INTRODUCTION

A wealth of literature already exists on contemporary U.S.
policy in the Persian Gulf and Arabian Peninsula. Most of this literature, both published and unpublished, has focused on a few important issues: the nature and evolution of U.S. interests in the
region; U.S. dependence on gulf oil; superpower rivalries and military posturing in the Persian Gulf/Indian Ocean regions; regional
security; successes and failures of U.S. policies; the "loss" of Iran
and the rise of Islamic fundamentalism; present and future stability
in the region; and the impact of such stability on the future conduct
of U.S. policy toward the area.

The policy studies that have appeared in the United States since
the mid-1970s, whether published by university presses, commercial
publishers, or policy ("think-tank") institutes, have mostly supported
a few basic tenets of U.S. policy in the gulf. These tenets state that
because of U.S. dependence on gulf oil, Washington is vitally commit-
ed to maintaining a "secure" gulf and therefore cannot stand idly by
in the event that gulf security is threatened. Also these studies have
not seriously questioned the basic thrust of the United States' Middle
East policy since the early 1970s: to secure the continued flow of
gulf oil, close and complex economic and military relationships have
had to be established with the states of the gulf.

Moreover, most of the literature, particularly those studies
and reports emanating from Washington, has reflected the U.S. administration's perception of the world and of the gulf. Whenever
this perception has changed, as it did between 1972 (the height of the
Shah's power) and 1979 (the Soviet invasion of Afghanistan), Washing-
ton-based or -commissioned studies have displayed a changing perception as well. It is possible to group this literature into three
categories. The first, and by far the largest category, encompasses
those studies with a status quo orientation. This group argues for a
continuation of present policies of United States-Persian Gulf military and economic cooperation as a guarantee of continued regional
security and stability. Some of these studies were written either by
former government officials with previous involvement in the making
of U.S. policy toward the gulf or by academics and journalists, who
were mostly supportive of and supported by gulf governments. In
either case, the studies have offered no more than apologias for existing policies.

The second category includes studies that, while supporting United States-Persian Gulf cooperation, have generally recommended an active interest on the part of Washington in issues that might potentially threaten or undermine U.S. long-range interests in the gulf. Like the first category, studies in this group have also accepted Washington's definitions of U.S. interests and of such other concepts as gulf stability, security, and progress.

In the case of Iran for example, many of these studies pointed out the close relations with the Shah and Washington's unquestioned acceptance of the Shah's view of order, security, and progress in the region. The Shah's vision coincided extremely well with the so-called Nixon Doctrine in the early 1970s, thereby annointing the Shah as the policeman of the gulf and as a model of how the Nixon Doctrine was intended to function. Some of these studies questioned the wisdom of this U.S.-Iranian personal diplomacy, which focused on the Shah at a time when, particularly in the late 1970s, sociopolitical alienation in Iran began to work against the Shah.

Regarding the Arab side of the gulf, several studies again questioned Washington's personalized diplomacy. Such questioning reached a new high following the assassination of King Faisal in March 1975. On the positive side, some studies have recommended that the United States take a positive attitude toward Iraq and its leader Saddam Hussain, particularly after the signing of the Iraqi-Iranian agreement, which settled the Shatt al-Arab dispute in March 1975.

Similar recommendations continued to be made throughout the latter part of the 1970s, arguing that under the leadership of Saddam Hussain, Iraq was slowly but surely extricating itself from the Soviet orbit. It was argued that Iraq was adopting a more moderate posture in its relations with its gulf neighbors and in its oil-pricing policies within OPEC.

In the same vein, other studies encouraged Washington, especially in the aftermath of the disengagement agreements that former Secretary of State Henry Kissinger concluded between Israel and Egypt and Israel and Syria in 1974-75, to work toward a comprehensive resolution of the Palestinian conflict. These recommendations were supported by the argument that if Arab-U.S. relations in the gulf were to endure, such outstanding conflicts as the Palestinian question must be settled. As long as the conflict remains and as long as the United States is perceived to side with Israel regarding the continued occupation of Arab lands, the gulf Arab states will be reluctant to identify with U.S. economic and security policies in the region.

The third category of studies, by far the smallest of the three groups, includes those works that have addressed themselves to different kinds of issues from a different perspective. These studies, which have questioned the accepted definitions of such concepts as regional security and stability as being Western (primarily derived from the United States) in orientation and purpose, have argued that more attention should be paid to the view from within the gulf concerning what constitutes security for the countries of the region. Furthermore, it has been argued that if the United States expects to pursue its interests successfully, Washington must actively seek avenues of meaningful dialogue, which would lead through joint diplomatic endeavors, to resolution of the outstanding conflicts. Another argument made by an even fewer number of these studies is that gulf stability, as indeed elsewhere in the region, is directly linked to internal stability, which can only endure through a new kind of a working relationship between the peoples and their governments.

This book's basic thesis falls into the third category of studies. Several important questions are raised: What is the U.S. policy in the gulf? How is it made? How did it develop? And what are its successes and failures? In addition, the evolution of U.S. policy in the gulf since the late 1960s is traced, focusing on the process of policy making and on the content of policy.

Regional security is another major area examined in the book. Several vital questions will be addressed: What does security mean? Whose security is involved? Whose interests does it serve? If regional security is threatened, who should define the nature of such a threat? What action should be taken to neutralize such a threat and by whom? Can gulf security be realistically separated from internal stability? If it cannot, is internal stability synonymous with the continued survival of the regimes presently in power? If it is, what measures should be adopted by these regimes to preserve themselves?

Many gulf leaders have come to realize that neither a powerful military machine, nor a U.S. Navy over the horizon can ultimately help a ruler remain in power if an antiregime movement spreads in the country. While Washington cannot be oblivious to gulf security and stability, it would be foolish to flaunt its military presence or to impose its own definition of security on local states. U.S. military presence in the gulf region should be reexamined with a view toward less rhetoric, more credibility, a low-key presence, and a determined effort to continue a dialogue with the countries of the region. The United States should be cognizant of the view from within the gulf itself.

This view from within is examined in terms of specific issues: gulf security; gulf cooperation through the recently formed Gulf Cooperation Council; internal stability; and of course, United States' interest and policies toward both the gulf and the Arab-Israeli conflic

This internal view is in fact a combination of views expressed by gulf government officials, newspaper editorials, intellectuals (students and professors), and other reform-oriented persons. Permeating this book is a conscious effort to focus on the opinions of indigenous gulf leaders and elites, not those of expatriates.

The book presents two major challenges to U.S. policy makers. First, the realization that although as a superpower the United States can project its power throughout the Middle East, recent developments have taught us that Washington cannot control the destiny of the region. Local forces and leaders, including some of our closest friends, often act independently, with little, if any, regard for Washington's concerns or desires. Second, the inexorable linkage between U.S. interests in the gulf and the ongoing Palestine conflict necessitates that Washington's policy in the Persian Gulf/Arabian Peninsula region should be treated from a triangular perspective, with the United States contributing one side of the triangle. The other two sides are, of course, Israel and the Arab world.

As stated above, this book reflects many years of research in the gulf and many hours of interviews with gulf leaders from all walks of life. It also reflects an assessment of the internal dynamics of gulf societies—socially, politically, and economically—and the efforts of the leaders of these societies to build viable political communities that would be able to transcend the euphoria of oil-generated wealth and prominence.

THE PERSIAN GULF
AND
AMERICAN POLICY

Northwest Indian Ocean Area

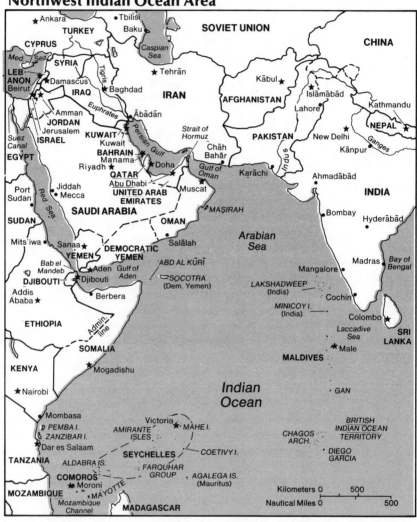

1

AN OVERVIEW

ISSUES AND AXIOMS

Events in the Middle East, and in the Persian Gulf in particular, continually remind us of the volatility of that region, of its threat to world peace, and of the United States' direct interest in that part of the world. Among these events, the following stand out:

The collapse of the Shah, the rise of the Islamic Republic, and the continued chaos in Iran.
The Soviet invasion of Afghanistan.
The continued conflict in Lebanon.
The Iraq-Iran war.
Israel's raid on the Iraqi nuclear reactor and its frequent threats to conduct preemptive strikes against its Arab neighbors.
The assassination of President Sadat.
Destabilizing plots in some gulf states.
The continued stalemate over the "autonomy" talks and the Saudi peace plan.

Most serious students of the Middle East and of U.S. foreign policy agree that bringing peace to this region is perhaps the most serious challenge facing the Reagan administration. They also agree on several other major points, which are considered somewhat axiomatic for this presentation:

1. The present state of tension in the region cannot continue for long without erupting into further violence with the potential of superpower involvement.

1

2. Although as a superpower the United States has the capability of projecting its power throughout the Middle East, recent developments have taught us that Washington cannot control the destiny of that region. As mentioned above, local forces and leaders, including some of our closest allies, often act independently, with little, if any, regard for Washington's concerns or desires.

3. Washington's interests and policies toward the Mideast, particularly the Persian Gulf, cannot be viewed in isolation from the interests and concerns of the peoples and governments of that area. These interests transcend those of any one country in the region and therefore to be served more effectively, Washington's approach must become more demonstrably evenhanded.

4. While it was psychologically uplifting for the U.S. public in January 1980 to hear President Carter announce the so-called "Carter Doctrine," it became painfully apparent to the friendly governments in the region that Carter's statement lacked both purpose and power. The Rapid Deployment Force, which was supposed to be the major tool of the Carter Doctrine, soon fell prey to interservice squabbling.

5. Although the United States should be commended for its great efforts in concluding a peace agreement between Israel and Egypt, the Camp David Framework for Peace has had little success concerning the Palestine question. A more imaginative approach is needed if a lasting peace is to be achieved. The traditional U.S. policy of maintaining harmonious relations with both Israel and the Arab world is rapidly becoming an impossible balancing act that can no longer guarantee regional stability.

6. Although gulf governments believe that maintaining gulf security is their responsibility, and although steps toward regional cooperation have been recently taken, particularly in the form of the Gulf Cooperation Council, most of these governments still look toward Washington for protection against any threat to their security. A continuing dichotomy is of course the one between U.S. protection and U.S. presence. The "over-the-horizon" presence might be adequate only in the short term. The serious definitional disagreements of such key concepts as security and stability have often complicated U.S. relations with the countries of the region. Such concepts cannot be meaningfully defined without a continued dialogue with U.S. allies in the area.

7. Gulf leaders perceive U.S. security policy toward the gulf as confused, vague, and often contradictory. This was particularly true during the last year of the Carter administration (specifically in relation to the Carter Doctrine, the Rapid Deployment Force, and the sale of sophisticated arms).

8. In discussing gulf security and U.S. direct interest in it, one notices two basic linkages. One linkage exists between regional security and internal stability within the countries themselves. The other inexorable link exists between the Palestinian conflict and future stability. On the internal level, future stability will be directly affected by such factors as political participation, modernization, demography, and border conflicts. The other linkage is a triangular one involving the United States, the Persian Gulf, and Israel. While solving the Palestine/Israel conflict would not eliminate the other elements of instability, it would substantially help to establish a more conducive environment for the pursuit of U.S. interests. In the final analysis, however, regional stability is inexorably linked to the internal stability of the regimes themselves.

9. No peace arrangement in the Middle East will endure unless the Palestinian conflict is resolved. Any such resolution must by definition include the Palestinians through direct and genuine Palestinian participation. Bilateral peace agreements should be supported; however, they are no substitute for a real durable peace.

10. Since it is impossible to negotiate with 4 million Palestinians, negotiations must be accomplished through the leadership, which so far has been vested in the Palestine Liberation Organization. Refusal to talk with a conflicting party is both unreasonable and impractical; it also runs counter to the traditional U.S. principle of negotiation.

11. To endure, peace in the Middle East must recognize the existence of all states, including Israel, and the principle of self-determination of all peoples, including the Palestinians.

12. Finally, peace in the Middle East is not only good for U.S. moral sensibilities, it is also good for Washington's national interest.

THE SETTING

Before plunging into policy particulars, it is instructive to note that the Arabian Peninsula/Persian Gulf region is a peculiarly complex part of the Middle East. Although it is impossible to isolate the gulf from the rest of the region—politically, economically, or strategically—the geopolitical characteristics of the gulf can be examined separately. The countries under discussion are of course: three relatively large ones (Iran, Iraq, and Saudi Arabia) and five small ones (Kuwait, Bahrain, Qatar, the United Arab Emirates, and Oman). Seven of the eight are Arab, while the eighth (Iran), which is by far the largest, is a non-Arab state.

Physically, gulf countries spread across an area of over 1.8 million square miles and include a population of over 60 million people (see Table 1.1). The area is bordered by Afghanistan in the east, the Soviet Union in the north, the Red Sea in the west, and the Arabian Sea and Indian Ocean in the south. The region is mostly desert, with oil as the main natural resource. Indeed, it is because of oil that this region has acquired its international significance. Of the eight countries, only Iran and Iraq are potentially self-sufficient in agriculture. However, the entire region suffers from limited water resources.

Gulf states are all Muslim oil-rich states, which have developing economies and relatively sparse populations. Aside from Iraq and Iran, which have a relative abundance of arable land and water resources and are potentially self-supporting in agricultural products, the other states possess mainly desert lands with an arid climate and a poor agricultural sector. These societies import practically all of their agricultural needs.

Among the Arab states, Iraq is at a comparatively advanced stage of industrial development, particularly in terms of experience, trained manpower, long-term planning, and availability of resources and manpower, while the other states are still in the initial stages of industrialization.

Although the Arab states possess a similar cultural heritage, in terms of racial origin, religious affiliation, and social configurations, their populations are often vastly dissimilar. The first major demographic observation that must be made concerns the makeup of the population. This is significant in terms of both social development and the composition of the country's labor force. In this area, Iraq and Iran are again different from the other states in that they are relatively labor sufficient. The other states, although rich in capital, have had to rely on hundreds of thousands of foreign workers. This expatriate reservoir of manpower will continue to be sorely needed in Saudi Arabia, Kuwait, Qatar, Oman, and the United Arab Emirates for the remainder of the century. This phenomenon is a reflection of two basic facts: the lack of trained indigenous manpower in these states; and the presence of large nonindigenous minorities. Hence, the small size of the indigenous population in these countries is incapable of producing a large enough workforce to power the ambitious economic projects approved for implementation. The political fallout of these economic facts cannot be overemphasized.

Again excepting Iraq (in which the nonindigenous population constitutes an infinitesimal percentage of the total population), the nonindigenous population in the other states is estimated at 40 percent in Saudi Arabia (primarily Yemenis and, most recently, Southeast Asians), 60 percent in Kuwait (mostly Palestinians and to a

TABLE 1.1

The Arabian Peninsula and the Persian Gulf: Basic Facts

Country	Area (sq. m.)	Population (est.)			Religion		GNP/Capita (in U.S. dollars)	GNP (est.) (in billions)
		Total (in thousands)	Indigenous (percent)	Alien (percent)	Sunni (percent)	Shi'a (percent)		
Bahrain	260	360	78.0	22.0	44.3	47.9	2,500	1.5
Iran	636,363	38,000	100.0	0	9.8	88.2	2,170	76.0
Iraq	172,000	13,230	98.4	0.6	40.5	52.5	1,550	22.7
Kuwait	7,780	1,340	47.7	52.3	84.6	10.4	15,480	18.0
Oman	82,030	900	90.0	10.0	25.0	50.0*	2,570	2.2
Qatar	4,000	220	19.0	81.0	70.3	24.3	12,740	2.8
Saudi Arabia	873,000	7,870	78.6	21.4	92.1	5.0	10,000	63.0
United Arab Emirates	32,280	800	25.0	75.0	62.5	15.0	14,230	11.0

*Ibadis. About 19 percent of the Omani population is Christian.
Source: Compiled by the author.

lesser extent Pakistanis and Indians), and over 66 percent in the United Arab Emirates (mostly Iranians and Pakistanis and, to a lesser extent, Indians). This latter percentage also applies to Qatar.

The picture becomes more striking when one examines the labor force in these countries. In a 1975 estimate, the percentage of nationals to nonnationals in the labor force was 57.0 to 43.0 in Saudi Arabia, 30.6 to 69.4 in Kuwait, and 15.2 to 84.8 in the United Arab Emirates. In Qatar, the percentage of the nationals to the nonnationals in the labor force in 1975 was 18.9 to 81.1. The ethnic origin of the migrant workers in these states is also revealing. Again using the same estimates for 1975, the majority of migrant workers in Kuwait (69 percent) and in Saudi Arabia (90 percent) was Arab, while in the United Arab Emirates the majority (65 percent) was Asian. It is now estimated that in the 1980s and 1990s the percentage of Arab workers in the capital-rich states will drop considerably and be replaced primarily by Southeast Asian workers.[1]

Another social factor of significance in the Persian Gulf is, of course, religion. Although all gulf states adhere to the Islamic faith and although all of them, other than Iran, are ruled by Sunni Muslims, their perception of the role of Islam in the affairs of state varies significantly from state to state. It was a fact, for example, that Saudi Arabia's foreign policy, particularly during the reign of King Faisal from 1964 to 1975, was principally influenced by Islam. This was manifested in Saudi Arabia's foreign aid to Islamic states (mostly Asian and African) and by King Faisal's strong position on Jerusalem and its centrality to the Palestinian conflict. Domestically, Islam was also the foundation of the social-legal fabric of the Saudi polity.

Saudi Arabia and Iran are ranked on the top of the scale of adherence to Islam as a guide to government, while Qatar comes second, the United Arab Emirates and Oman third, Bahrain and Kuwait fourth, and Iraq fifth. Secularism in this context is only a matter of degree and in no way conveys the meaning associated with the term in Western political systems. While on this scale, Iraq appears to be more secular than its gulf neighbors, Iraqi regional relations have suffered from another religious constraint. Over 50 percent of Iraq's population is of the Shi'a faith, which is the same faith that a vast majority of the Iranian people adheres to. Accordingly, the Shi'a-Sunni tension has been a serious factor in inter- and intra-gulf relations. Historically, particularly in gulf countries, the Shi'a-Sunni split has always had political overtones.

Unlike its Arab gulf neighbors, Iraq does not have a large nonindigenous minority, but it does have an indigenous non-Arab minority of Kurds, who constitute just under 20 percent of the population. Arab-Kurdish relations within the country have been violent. The protracted conflict has been costly both in human terms and in physical resources. Furthermore, until the Iraqi-Iranian rapprochement in March 1975, the Kurdish question was a major national issue in Iraq, which might be resurrected in the future.

Modernization is another area that must be examined as part of the general setting of Persian Gulf societies. Several specific questions should be raised. If modernization implies a transformation from a traditional society to a modern political and social polity, how can one explain the apparent linkage between the modernizing process and family rule? Does the process of modernization in traditional societies carry within it the seeds of inevitable disruptions of the political process and conflict within the body politic? If so, how can these disruptions be contained? What does the Iranian experience, unique as it may be, portend for neighboring gulf societies? Will the modernizing process abet or hinder the establishment of open government, or are the political systems of the gulf doomed to the rule of force? Will these governments be able to establish institutions based on legitimate authority and capable of transcending specific leaders, regardless of how charismatic they may be?

Modernization has affected the entire political, economic, and social fabric of these societies. It has been accomplished by governmental policies supported by the ruling families, implemented by a bureaucratic cadre of technocrats, and pushed forward by the wealthy entrepreneurs and businessmen. Modernization has also been strongly supported by the country's news media, particularly the very few privately owned daily and weekly newspapers.

While social and economic institutions have supported modernization policies, the political systems lag somewhat behind. The political structure continues to be pyramidal and hierarchical; power flows from a ruling family that occupies the apex of the pyramid.

The nonfamily but influential stratum of the population that supports the policies of modernization occupies the layer immediately below the apex. This stratum of influential families, businessmen, and wealthy merchants see their support of these policies as a function of the rewards they reap from the system. They are beneficiaries of family rule, and they perceive themselves as true capitalists in support of a private enterprise system.

Below these two relatively small segments lies a large stratum that has barely felt the positive impact of modernization. This layer consists primarily of low-level civil servants, teachers, unskilled workers (mainly in construction and services), fishermen, small grocers, farmers, and nomads. This sector of the population lives in a world alien to that of wealth, modern society, and contemporary fashion. Whatever rewards members of this stratum receive from the system come in the form of paternalistic gifts such as public housing, if available, medical treatment in government hospitals, and education.

Once the negative effects of rapid modernization, such as inflation, high prices, and exorbitant housing costs, begin to affect their daily lives and livelihood, in what ways will they vent their anger? Will they turn to an underground movement of ideologues? Or will they turn to their mullas (a Shi'a priest) to renounce all modernization as the work of the devil?

These states will most likely experience heightened tension and perhaps political instability in their attempts to modernize. However, the possibility of evolutionary modernization does exist; each country, through its emerging political system, seems to have the major ingredients for a relatively peaceful modernization.

An important institution in terms of social modernization is obviously Islam, which on the whole has resisted modernization. While Islam as a church has undergone traumatic changes since World War II and while it had lost its legitimacy as a system of government until recently, "Islamic awareness" continues to be a powerful force in gulf societies. It is fair to say that a serious identity conflict exists in Arab society as a whole between Muslims and their religion. To illustrate, the modernizing Muslim tends to be secular in training, perception, ideology, and world view. However, Islam is accepted as the official religion in practically every Arab state. A reference to this is invariably found in most Arab constitutions in the first half dozen articles. Even though the formal Islamic political structure has disintegrated in this century, Islam as a way of life has survived in the Arabs' perception of themselves and their values. This conflict between the modernizing Muslim and Islam will contribute to the tensions marring the modernizing process.

Political ideology of the regime and political culture of the society will also continue to influence political development in the gulf. These countries have exhibited an astounding range of governmental forms, from absolute monarchy to considerable chaos, with most of the regimes falling in the category of authoritarian centralized government. The Saudi Arabian and Iranian political systems function according to the dictates of Islam. The Saudis follow the tenets of orthodox Sunni Islam as perceived by them in the Koran, while Iran is ruled by the Shi'a clerical hierarchy according to the Constitution of the Islamic Republic of Iran.

Although all states are ruled by authoritarian regimes, Iraq differs from the others in the sources of its authoritarianism. The Iraqi socialist regime derives its authority to rule from the Ba'th party in the form of the Revolutionary Command Council, which was

controlled by President Hasan al-Bakr and his formidable deputy
Saddam Hussein. Upon the resignation of President al-Bakr in the
summer of 1979, Vice-President Hussein took command. The political-
cal culture of the Iraqi polity is measured by teachings of the Ba'th
party, as enunciated by the leadership and by the founder of the
party, Michel 'Aflaq, who is presently residing in Baghdad.

The other small states, while different in the actual exercise
of power, are solidly based on tribalism as expressed in family-
centered rule. The ruling families, while deriving their authority
from classical Islam, have been able to initiate a cautious process
of economic, social, and bureaucratic modernization. In Saudi
Arabia, for example, this process involves a myriad of economic
and administrative policies and thousands of highly educated technocrats, who are not necessarily members of the ruling family. So
far the process has worked; however, new stresses and strains are
beginning to be felt in the body politic.

Kuwait, the first of the gulf amirates to become independent
in 1961, is ruled by the al-Sabah family in an authoritarian but semi-
open fashion. To their credit, a constitution was promulgated in
1962, and a semielected National Assembly was convened in the
same year. However, the inevitable tension between popular participation in government and a strong family rule led ultimately to
the dissolution of the assembly in 1976. Early in 1979 Kuwait's
rulers indicated that the National Assembly would be reinstituted
through an election, which was accomplished in early 1981.

As noted earlier, Kuwait has a large minority of Palestinians
and has been sensitive to developments regarding the Palestine-
Israel conflict. Hence, it can be asserted that in addition to what
some see as a basic contradiction between open government and
authoritarian family rule, several outside factors contributed to the
dissolution of the Kuwaiti National Assembly. Among these are the
post-1975 trend to the right in the gulf and Saudi Arabia's dislike
for participatory government. It has persistently counselled its
neighbors against moving too fast too soon in opening up the regimes.
Finally, there was a perceived fear on the part of the Kuwaiti leadership that popular opposition to the Egyptian-Israeli Peace Treaty
and the U.S. support of Israel might produce acrimonious wrangles
in the National Assembly, and that such debates might harm Kuwaiti
foreign relations. Several newspapers and magazines in Kuwait
were also ordered to cease publication for different periods of time.
It would be noted that Bahrain, which had modeled its constitutional
system on that of Kuwait, had dissolved its National Assembly a
year earlier, in August 1975. The official reason given was the government's (ruling family's) inability to work further with the "leftist"
members of the National Assembly.

The United Arab Emirates established its own form of federal structure in late 1971. The six original amirates (Abu Dhabi, Dubai, Sharja, Um al-Qaywayn, 'Ajman, and Fujayra), were joined in February 1972 by Ra's al-Khayma. The federation is still ruled by Shaikh Zayed of Abu Dhabi, which is the richest and most populous of the amirates. The federation has had its share of troubles and crises; Dubai, the second richest amirate, has even threatened to withdraw from the federation. However, its ruler, Shaikh Rashed, has always been convinced to stay in the federation, often by grants of financial aid and political power from Abu Dhabi. The 1976 crisis, when the conflict between Abu Dhabi and D'ubai became open, has been the most threatening to the existence of the federation. After seeking to resign, Shaikh Zayed was finally convinced to stay and serve another term. Kuwaiti mediation played a positive role in containing the crisis.

The United Arab Emirates operates under a provisional constitution through a federal machinery based on three key components: the Supreme Council, the Cabinet, and the Federal National Council. The Supreme Council is composed of the rulers of the seven amirates. The Cabinet has been composed of technocrats, although the character of the Cabinet is expected to change since Shaikh Rashed of Dubai was recently appointed its head. The Federal National Council is composed of 40 members, mostly from the smaller amirates (six each from Sharja and Ra's al-Khayma, four each from Um al-Qaywayn, 'Ajman, and Fujayra, and eight each from Abu Dhabi and Dubai). Because of the continued tension within the federation, caused by Dubai's jockeying for power, most of the federal machinery has not been terribly effective. Although to a casual observer these problems might seem to be primarily domestic, they have been at the center of the U.A.E.'s relations with its neighbors. Saudi Arabia and Kuwait have often been involved in mediation, and Shaikh Rashed has often carried on his own foreign relations with Iran, India, and other powers. The smaller amirates have basically done whatever they could get away with.

Extremes in wealth and poverty exist in every Persian Gulf country. Wealth is largely retained in the hands of the governing and entrepreneurial elites, while the middle class is barely emerging. An economic system of state capitalism permeates most of the countries of the region, with the ruling families, particularly in the oil countries, receiving the largest share.

Strategically, the entire area is of unparalleled importance to both superpowers. It provides a tempting array of oil resources, warm-water ports, and strategic waterways. However, the United States is 7,000 miles away, while the gulf region is in the Soviet Union's backyard.

Given these factors, it is small wonder that the region has so many internal factors of potential instability. Chief among these factors are the lack of popular political participation, the Palestinian conflict, and regional security. Although these issues are treated at length below, it is possible to see in this overview how, together with oil, they have directly affected relations among gulf states and between these states and the outside world.

RELATIONS AMONG GULF STATES

Gulf states cannot escape being pushed into the limelight of world politics for long, since oil, the Palestinian conflict, and regional security are both regional and international issues, and they directly involve major powers and even the superpowers. Furthermore, it is expected that these same key issues will pervade future relations and will, to varying degrees, dictate the nature of political and economic developments in gulf states for the remainder of this century. Because of these and other related issues, gulf states will therefore find themselves operating within at least four concentric circles simultaneously and with much more intensity than in the past: the gulf circle; the Arab circle; the Islamic circle; and the international (superpower) circle.

It is clear that the issues of oil and Palestine will interact throughout the four circles directly and indirectly, diplomatically and militarily, and will be crucial in the behavior of gulf states toward other states or organizations within any of the four circles. Accordingly, perhaps to the discomfort of the gulf states, relations among these states, even those in a purely gulf context, such as the recently established Gulf Cooperation Council, will hardly escape being noticed internationally. Present international realities are such that a fundamental trilateral linkage exists between the politics of Palestine, the politics of oil, and of course the international policies of the industrial world. As has been demonstrated since the October 1973 war, the organic nature of this linkage simply means that a disruption in one of the three parties will affect the other two.

Early in the 1970s, prior to the October War and the linking of oil and politics, relations among gulf states were significantly governed by political ideology and by the perceptions of the leaders of those states of what constituted the ideological bases of their political system. Ideology in this context focused on three areas: the nature of the regime, the perception of gulf security and who protected or threatened that security, and relations with outside powers, particularly the United States and the Soviet Union.

Although post-World War II strategic planning of the super-powers did include the gulf regions, most of the Arab littoral coast was under British protection. It wasn't until the 1960s and early 1970s that new states appeared. Secondly, it was not until the question of energy reached crisis proportions in the early 1970s that the gulf began to cast an ominous shadow in the planning of the industrial world. In retrospect, it seemed incredible that only a few years ago the industrial world assumed that oil would always be available at very cheap prices. The October War and the subsequent oil embargo very dramatically ended that myth. Suddenly the protection of the gulf became of strategic importance to the West, particularly the United States. Iran under the Shah was anointed under the Nixon Doctrine as the guardian of the gulf. Simultaneously, the United States under the direction of former Secretary of State Kissinger began to investigate the new, volatile, and unpredictable merger of the politics of oil and the politics of Palestine. Saudi Arabia became the target of Kissinger's diplomatic attempts to solve the Palestinian conflict. Concómitant with the search for that illusive peace, the United States embarked on a new search for the more tangible petrodollars. Fortunately for the United States and unfortunately for the region, Kissinger's policy succeeded in the latter goal but failed in the former.

In their relations with each other, gulf states could not escape the effects of new developments and became embroiled in this complex triangular relationship of oil, Palestine, and regional security. The fall of the Shah in January 1979 was, however, only one of several traumas that have affected the gulf states in the latter part of the 1970s. In order to place these other developments in their proper perspective, it might be useful to view briefly the different periods through which relations among gulf states have passed.

It is generally accepted that contemporary relations among gulf states started in 1968, when the British government announced its intention to withdraw from the east of Suez by the end of 1971. Since several major developments transpired in the gulf between 1968 and 1979, it might be convenient to subdivide the entire decade into five different periods: 1968-late 1971; 1972-late 1973; 1974-spring 1975; mid-1975-1979; and late 1979-present.

Between 1968 and 1971 the main efforts of gulf states focused on formulating an independent political future for the amirates and on protecting their independent existence against any threats, actual or potential, internal or external. Since Iraq was in the midst of consolidating its own Ba'thist regime, it was not involved in this process at all. The nine amirates of the lower gulf (the seven that later joined into the U.A.E. plus Bahrain and Qatar) met for a period of almost three years, hoping to produce an acceptable united state for all of them. The desire to establish a federal state resulted from a realization of the weakness of their existence as separate states. Several formulas were reviewed, but none were implemented. Both Saudi Arabia and Kuwait offered to mediate differences among the rulers of the various amirates. However, the final result was that by late 1971 Bahrain and Qatar declared themselves independent states. Almost simultaneously, the United Arab Emirates came into existence, also as a separate state.

The shadow of Iran's territorial claims to Bahrain hovered over the federation talks, but thanks to United States', British, and United Nations diplomacy, Iran renounced its claim to Bahrain, thereby paving the way for the latter's independence. However, in late 1971 Iran occupied three gulf islands (the two Tunbs and Abu Musa). The Iranian action produced protests on the Arab side of the gulf, including Iraq, Saudi Arabia, and Kuwait, but to no avail. As of this writing, the islands remain under Iranian control.

In the 1972-73 period, gulf states were preoccupied with internal developments; this was reflected in their relations with each other. Iraq focused on three areas: the nationalization of its oil industry; the consolidation of its Ba'thist regime under the leadership of Hasan al-Bakr; and the Kurdish rebellion in the northern part of the country.

On the gulf front, Iraq was embroiled in a boundary dispute with Kuwait and with Iran. Iraq also extended assistance to liberation movements in the region, particularly the Popular Front for the Liberation of Oman and the Arabian Gulf (PFLOAG), which operated out of South Yemen against the sultan of Oman and other tribal regimes. In addition, Iraq established strong relations with the Soviet Union and came to be viewed by its neighbors, including Iran and Saudi Arabia, as a Soviet proxy in the region working against regional status quo stability. Consequently, its relations with its neighbors cooled considerably, which was a condition that lasted for at least three years. However, contrary to the expectations of many, Iraq did succeed in its nationalization confrontation with the oil companies, even though its oil-rich neighbors opted for gradual participation agreements, rather than total control.

Saudi Arabia was preoccupied with the implementation of King Faisal's ten-point domestic reform program. At the same time, the Saudi government made it clear to its neighbors that: its foreign policy was based on Islam; it opposed communism; it saw Soviet designs in the region; it supported family rule in neighboring states; and supported efforts to combat underground "leftist" and "alien" movements. Furthermore, Saudi Arabia did not necessarily disapprove of the United States' interpretation of regional stability/instability in the gulf. Saudi Arabia even encouraged a more active U.S. role in the area.

The Arab-Israeli War in October 1973 shattered many preconceived relationships. The oil embargo supported by the Organization of Arab Petroleum Exporting Countries (OAPEC) and the phenomenal increases in the price of crude oil have strengthened the relations among gulf states despite their ideological differences. More importantly, the oil embargo reflected unanimous agreement on the part of the Arab gulf states on three major points: oil was to be used as a political weapon; the weapon was to be used in support of the Palestinian people and against Israel and the United States; and the purpose of using the weapon was to force Washington to take a more active role in solving the Arab-Israeli conflict. In supporting the oil embargo, Saudi Arabia emerged as a regional power, which was a role that its Arab neighbors encouraged. Accordingly, Saudi relations with other Arab gulf states in the postembargo period reflected Saudi Arabia's expanding role in Arab, regional, Islamic, and international affairs. In addition, Saudi Arabia became a major actor in the Arab-Israeli conflict by becoming Egypt's main financier—until 1978.

During 1974 and 1975, Saudi Arabia supported Egypt's troop disengagement agreements with Israel and began to develop warm and complex economic, financial, and military relations with the United States. Neighboring amirates supported the new Saudi-United States connection, but Iraq was very critical of it. Yet, it can be argued that since 1974 political relations among Arab gulf states have become more friendly and pragmatic. The Iraqi-Iranian agreement in March 1975 over the Shatt al-'Arab estuary practically eliminated the Kurdish problem for Iraq.

Iraq began to look southward to establish closer relations with its neighbors. In the meantime, Iraq has halted its support of the Popular Front for the Liberation of Oman, thereby contributing to ending the Dhofari rebellion. As a result, Saudi-Iraqi relations have become close, as have Iraqi relations with Kuwait and the rest of the amirates. Iraq's disagreement with the Soviet Union has contributed further to the warming relations in the gulf.

The assassination of King Faisal in March 1975 and the rise of King Khalid and Prince Fahd to power did not alter Saudi relations with neighboring states. Reflecting on the 1974-76 period, it can be stated that the Arab states of the gulf almost unanimously supported oil price rises, oil production cuts, and the political gains of the Palestine Liberation Organization. They also continued to be suspicious of the Shah's role in the gulf. This situation prevailed through early 1979.

The first major event in this period, which shook the Arab world to its foundations, was President Sadat's visit to Israel in November 1977. While Iraq and Kuwait openly condemned the Sadat peace initiative, Saudi Arabia and the other amirates adopted a more cautious wait-and-see attitude. Their silence was chiefly based on the promises made by Sadat and later by the United States that Sadat's initiative was aimed at a comprehensive peace agreement, not as a separate Egyptian-Israeli Peace Treaty. However, the signing of the Camp David Peace Accords in September 1978 and particularly the signing of the Egyptian-Israeli Peace Treaty in March 1979 were condemned throughout the Arab world as a betrayal on the part of the Egyptian leadership. Saudi Arabia, together with most of the Arab countries, attended the Baghdad summit in March 1979 and joined in the unanimous condemnation of President Sadat. Saudi Arabia also participated in the economic and political sanctions adopted at the Baghdad summit against Egypt. Thus, through their common opposition to Sadat, Saudi Arabia, Iraq, Kuwait, the United Arab Emirates, Bahrain, and Qatar have maintained relations that are much warmer than earlier in the decade. Of the gulf states, only Oman openly supported Egypt's quest for peace with Israel.

Aside from the above-mentioned patterns of political relations, Arab gulf states have also established a promising foundation for economic and security cooperation. While this type of cooperation is still nascent in terms of long-range planning and while it has yet to be translated into tangible benefits for the peoples of the region, it is possible to be guardedly optimistic about the future of the region, even after the oil is depleted, if the right political atmosphere should prevail.

The development of political relations among gulf states since the early 1970s indicates clearly that, while some positive factors can be discerned for the future, many outside factors will also determine these relations. Although the gulf states will continue to be influential in the international arena, they do not have much control over the superpowers in their plans to establish spheres of influence. Similarly, gulf states might be able to control the flow and prices of oil, but the so-called oil weapon is a double-edged sword. Malaise in the economies of the industrial world or a significant drop in oil consumption would be quickly felt in the oil-producing countries as well. Paradoxically, even though these states have become influential members of the world nation-state system, their rising prestige has often been a mixed blessing. Being at the center of the world's economic stage has not enhanced their independence. On the contrary, primacy in the industrial world's economies has confirmed their dependence on the industrial nations—economically, politically, and militarily. Even in the area of labor migration, the gulf states find themselves in a complex interdependent relationship with the developing countries as well.

On the question of Palestine, the linkage of oil and politics has only a limited effectiveness in producing a peaceful settlement acceptable to Israel, the Palestinians, the United States, and the Soviet Union. Nor do they have any ability to influence the unfolding of events in Iran or the long-range direction of its revolutionary Islamic government. Indeed, the protracted Iraq-Iran war amply illustrates the gulf states' impotence in resolving even purely gulf issues.

From an optimistic viewpoint, gulf states have already established a strong precedent for cooperation and friendly relations. On the Arab side of the gulf, the eruption in Iran and the general unpredictability of dependence on outside powers seem to have drawn those states together strategically and even ideologically closer. Their common interest in the region's collective security and their realization of the benefits of collective economic planning are hopeful indicators of cooperative regional relations both economically and politically.

The only other ingredient lacking for stable relations among these states is the political involvement of their own peoples in building a viable gulf community. If a peaceful way could be found to involve the people of the gulf in their own governments, the outlook for regional stability would markedly improve.

EVOLUTION OF U.S. POLICY IN THE GULF

The U.S. concern for Mideast stability, the possibility of Soviet threats, and the need for gulf oil have led to several major statements on the part of U.S. presidents. Four such statements or doctrines have been advanced with varying degrees of clarity and effectiveness: The Truman Doctrine (March 12, 1947); the Eisenhower Doctrine (January 5, 1957); the Nixon Doctrine (February 18, 1970); and the Carter Doctrine (January 23, 1980). The first, second, and fourth doctrines focused directly on "communist" threats to states and established regimes in the area. All four of the doctrines committed the United States to respond directly or through local states if any threat, presumably communist, were to occur or if the United States were invited to respond by any state in the area. The Truman, the Eisenhower, and the Carter Doctrines have prescribed a direct U.S. involvement, whereas the Nixon Doctrine called for action by local states using U.S. weapons but not U.S. soldiers. The operative principles of the Nixon Doctrine were partnership, strength, and willingness to negotiate: "Peace through partnership." The following statements offer a synopsis of the four doctrines:

President Truman on Communist aggression in Greece and Turkey:

> It must be the policy of the United States to support free peoples who are resisting attempted subjugation by armed minorities or by outside pressures. We must assist free peoples to work out their destinies in their own way. Our help should be primarily through economic and financial aid which is essential to economic stability and orderly political processes. [2]

President Eisenhower on a Communist threat to Middle Eastern countries and on authorizing the United States to do the following:

> To cooperate with and assist any nation or groups of nations in the Middle East in the development of economic strength dedicated to the maintenance of national independence. To undertake in the same region programs of military assistance and cooperation with any nation or groups of nations which desires such aid. To include the employment of armed forces of the United States to secure and protect the territorial integrity and political independence of such nations, requesting such aid, against overt armed aggression from any nation controlled by international communism. [3]

President Nixon on the limits of U.S. power and commitment to help other nations:

> The United States will participate in the defense and development of allies and friends, but that America cannot—and will not—conceive all the plans, design all the programs, execute all the decisions and undertake all the defense of the free nations of the world. We will help where it makes a real difference and is considered in our interest. [4]

President Carter on the Soviet threat to the Persian Gulf:

> Let our position be absolutely clear: An attempt by any outside force to gain control of the Persian Gulf region will be regarded as an assault on the vital interests of the United States of America, and such an assault will be repelled by any means necessary, including military force. [5]

The above statements indicate that successive presidents have perceived the Middle East to be vital to U.S. national interest, that regional stability must be maintained, and that the United States would not be oblivious to any threat to stability in the area. The Truman Doctrine was implemented successfully in Greece and Turkey through U.S. economic and military aid. The Eisenhower Doctrine was never implemented, primarily because no Middle Eastern country ever called on the United States to invoke this doctrine.

The Nixon Doctrine's application in the Middle East was dramatically illustrated in Washington's support of the Shah as the policeman of the gulf. However, the collapse of the Shah, the increasing U.S. dependence on gulf oil, the revolution in Iran, and the Soviet invasion of Afghanistan have convinced U.S. policy makers that protection by proxy is unpredictable, and that to protect its strategic interest in the gulf, the United States might become increasingly involved directly. This direct involvement is the cornerstone of the Carter Doctrine.

It is interesting that from 1947 to 1980, U.S. presidents felt an increasing need to clearly define the area that they perceived as vital to U.S. national security and strategic interest. President Truman's message applied to Greece and Turkey, two non-Arab states. President Eisenhower's message applied mainly to the Fertile Crescent states, particularly those that felt threatened by the rising tide of Nasser's Arab nationalism. President Nixon changed the focus from the Fertile Crescent to the Persian Gulf, and this change was dramatically sharpened by President Carter.

In the 1950s and 1960s, the Arab-Israeli conflict was essentially limited to Israel and the Arab states; Israel won whenever the conflict erupted into open warfare. Palestinian nationalism was dormant, oil was available in unlimited quantities at very low prices, and the policies of oil were largely determined by the oil companies, not by the oil-producing countries. This picture changed dramatically in the 1970s: Palestinian nationalism emerged as an international factor; oil became a political weapon; oil companies were replaced as policy makers by the producing states through OPEC; the continued availability of oil to the industrial world at reasonable prices became problematical; and an Arab desire for an accommodation with Israel emerged. Washington advanced several specific policy objectives to fit the changing picture:

Commitment to the security of Israel.
Commitment to a comprehensive settlement of the Palestinian conflict.
Commitment to regional stability in the Arabian Peninsula and gulf region.

Support for gulf regional cooperation through a system of Arab-U.S.
and Iranian-U.S. partnerships in the gulf, with Saudi Arabia and
Iran being the two "pillars" of the partnership edifice.
Support for the continued availability of oil to the consuming countries.

By late 1975, it became apparent that new policies were required
in three of these areas: energy, the Palestinian conflict, and gulf
security. These areas then became the focus of the Carter administration's Mideast policy. Unfortunately, during the final months of
the Carter administration, U.S. foreign policy was perceived as
vacillating and lacking in leadership. The Carter administration's
reactions to the upheaval in Iran, to the Soviet invasion of Afghanistan,
and to Soviet threats in the gulf area left U.S. friends in the region
bewildered and unsure of Washington's resolve to resist Soviet aggression and of its determination to defend U.S. interests.

Leaders in Saudi Arabia and elsewhere in the gulf heard many
promises and exaggerated rhetoric from Carter, but they saw very
little action. The Carter Doctrine remained more words than substance.

Furthermore, the Carter administration failed to coordinate a
practical and effective policy with local leaders in the area to counteract the Soviet offensive. The administration also failed to develop
a credible military policy of its own, or with the European allies, to
demonstrate their commitment to resist Soviet aggression.

By way of illustration, gulf Arab leaders viewed Carter's response to the Soviet invasion of Afghanistan as being high on rhetoric
but low on action. They believed then that an embargo on grain ship-
ments to the Soviet Union and a boycott of the Olympics would be ineffective in forcing the Soviets out of Afghanistan. Other gulf leaders
also indicated that the conflicting statements from the Carter administration made gulf governments more uneasy regarding Washington's
position on Soviet advances in the Red Sea and Bab el Mandab regions.
How far, they asked, must the Soviets advance before Washington
would respond decisively?

Although the Reagan administration has attempted to create a
new image of U.S. concern and resolve in the gulf, by early 1982,
the Reagan administration had not developed a comprehensive political program for the region. Throughout 1981, the administration
did respond to urgent developments in the region, such as the assassination of President Anwar Sadat of Egypt. However, such a response
was only through _military_ aid and the deployment of U.S. forces. As
of the spring of 1982, no diplomatic program was articulated by the
administration to complement the military commitments that had
already been made to the Saudis and the Jordanians.

NOTES

1. J. S. Birks and C. A. Sinclair, "Economic and Social Implications of Current Development in the Arab Gulf: The Oriental Connection," in Social and Economic Development in the Arab Gulf, ed. Tim Niblock (London: Croom Helm, 1980), pp. 135-60.

2. Harry Truman, message to Congress, March 12, 1947. Quoted in Documents on the Middle East, ed. Ralph E. Magnus (Washington, D.C.: American Enterprise Institute, 1969), p. 66.

3. Dwight Eisenhower, message to Congress, January 5, 1957. Quoted in Documents on the Middle East, pp. 90-91.

4. Richard Nixon, annual report to Congress, February 18, 1969. Quoted in U.S. Foreign Policy for the 1970's: A New Strategy for Peace (Washington, D.C.: U.S. Government Printing Office, 1970), pp. 6-7.

5. Jimmy Carter, "The State of the Union," address to Congress on January 23, 1980. Quoted in Weekly Compilation of Presidential Documents, January 28, 1980, p. 197.

2

POLITICAL
PARTICIPATION

INTRODUCTION

The recent attempts of many gulf states to open up their political systems to popular participation recognize that internal stability
undergirds regional security. There is also a recognition that lack
of political participation is a major factor in potential instability,
one that must be addressed by those states if their present political
systems are to outlive any one current ruler.

There have been desultory efforts in this direction for a
decade, but the real impetus toward internal stability by popular
participation came from the demise of the Shah in January 1979.
The Shah's collapse was a sharp reminder that military might cannot keep a regime in power if the people desire otherwise. A military machine can neither create legitimacy nor generate the citizens' voluntary compliance with the law. The Islamic revolution
in Iran has forced Arab rulers to rethink their relationship with
their citizens. The popular revolution and the collapse of the
Pahlavi dynasty have been very traumatic for the ruling families
throughout the gulf region. The fact that an Islamic regime came
to power in Iran and that Islam is also the predominant religion in
neighboring Arab states has not been comforting, even to such a
staunchly religious state as Saudi Arabia.

The revolution in Iran has signaled neighboring states that
their internal security is problematical. While Saudi society, for
example, is drastically different from Iranian society and the conditions that led to the downfall of the Shah are not present in such
countries as Saudi Arabia, Kuwait, Qatar, the United Arab Emirates,
or Bahrain, it is always possible that internal dissent might some

day, perhaps fairly soon, erupt into violence. This in turn might threaten the existence of the familial regimes on the Arab side of the gulf. If this occurs, it is obvious that not only the Arab societies will be disturbed; the interests of many outside powers who rely on gulf oil will also be strongly affected. The most recent illustration of this point is the concern displayed by the international community in December 1981, when a small group of disaffected Bahrainis attempted to overthrow the government. Bahraini officials indicated that evidence was found linking the plot to Iran, but the significant fact is that those involved were indisputably Bahrainis. Of further significance is the evidence indicating that this attempt was but one of several planned disturbances in other gulf states, all of which involved local citizens.

The nature, topography, economics, and politics of the region make it very difficult to isolate any major development in a particular country and keep it from having a regional effect. Since this is the case, it is understandable that neighboring countries closely watched the disintegration of the Pahlavi dynasty and have followed developments within Iran under Khomeini with apprehension and anxiety.

The impact of the Iranian revolution on its Arab neighbors cannot be overemphasized. Most, if not all, of these societies are experiencing rapid change, both economically and socially; political repercussions are usually soon to follow. Sizable Iranian minorities are present in several Arab states (10 percent of the population in Bahrain and 20 percent in Qatar). This fact has influenced the ruling families' perceptions of events in Iran and of the long-term impact of these events on internal sociopolitical development in neighboring countries. The pivotal question is whether change in Arab gulf societies will be gradual and peaceful or if it will produce instability and violence. When a high-level Bahraini government official was asked his opinion on the Iranian revolution, he replied: "We had better go for democracy!" This tongue-in-cheek remark by a former supporter of the short-lived parliamentary experiment in Bahrain illustrates one aspect of the Bahraini reaction to the fall of the Shah.

A cursory examination of the political systems of the eight states under discussion indicates that they have approached questions of authority and legitimacy differently. Except for Iran and Iraq, gulf states are family-ruled, and political authority resides with the head of that family, who is variously titled amir, king, or sultan. Since early 1980, a belief seems to have emerged among some influential members of these families that for internal stability to endure a pragmatic and workable partnership must be forged between the peoples and their rulers.

In a series of articles in 1980 entitled "Democracy in the Gulf," The Middle East magazine examined the issue of popular participation in government in five gulf states: the United Arab Emirates, Kuwait, Bahrain, Qatar, and Saudi Arabia. The articles pointed to several common attitudes among the ruling camilies and leading elites of those countries regarding the question of popular participation.[1]

First, the legitimacy of any arrangement toward sharing power emanates from the Koranic/tribal principle of shura (consultation). This principle allows representatives of the community to express their views to the ruler but does not compel the ruler to abide by these views.

Second, although political authority and the "allocation of values" in the political systems of these states flow from the top to the bottom, the ruling families have more or less come to accept the usefulness of "opening up" their regimes for some sort of popular participation.

Third, because of the relatively small indigenous population in the gulf amirates and the rapid economic expansion, particularly since 1973, the lack of political participation has so far not caused major internal upheavals, but this situation is not expected to endure. The demands for political participation among the reform-oriented stratum of the population have been mostly moderate in tone and modest in objectives. Participation has been advocated by reformist groups in the context of continued family rule. It is interesting to note that these groups include businessmen, intellectuals, media executives, and high-level civil servants. They are bourgeois, indigenous, and beneficiaries of the present system.

Fourth, questions of authority and legitimacy based on centralized rule are far from settled. Most gulf societies are ruled by powerful families, which are a modern extension of an old tribal tradition. The reins of government are tightly held in the hands of the ruling family, which usually makes decisions on every major issue with minimal popular input into the decision-making process.

Fifth, while all gulf states have established a cabinet system of government, the ruler in most of them retains almost absolute power. Most of them, excluding Saudi Arabia and Oman, have written constitutions; only two family-ruled states, Bahrain and Kuwait, have implemented any sort of parliamentary system based on elections. Qatar and the United Arab Emirates continue to function under provisional constitutions. Indigenous political elites throughout the Arab states of the gulf have been speaking out, particularly since the Iranian revolution, for political reforms, including popular participation in government.

Sixth, a position seems to be developing within some ruling families that, if popular participation is channeled properly, it can be an asset to a regime and a stabilizing force in society.

Seventh, although a sympathetic response to demands for political participation is beginning to emerge among influential segments within the ruling families, the older, more traditional members of the inner family councils still believe that the familial atmosphere that binds the ruler and his people and the accessibility of the ruler to the people through the majlis are sufficient means of communication between citizens and government. Therefore, this renders a formal system of popular participation unnecessary.

The statements cited above have also indicated that one cannot deal meaningfully with questions of legitimacy, rule, and authority in any one amirate in isolation from the other amirates. They share several common characteristics: a family rule; a tribal/ Islamic tradition; a centralized authority; a relatively small territory, population, and administrative structure; and a rapidly expanding oil-based economy. Islam is both the underpinning of the political structure and the official religion of the state, and Islamic law is a primary source of legislation.

Regarding the constitutional foundation of government, it would be useful to highlight the following general observations:

First, although modern structures of government are being built in gulf amirates, authority has remained vested in an all-powerful ruling family.

Second, the move toward constitutional monarchy has not eliminated the tribal source of legitimacy. Furthermore, the rule is hereditary and the ruler's accession to power is not a matter of popular decision. While government is theoretically divided into executive, legislative, and judicial branches, the amir, as the chief executive, remains the source of legitimacy and authority. Members of the ruling family in each state also occupy the most important cabinet posts and other top government positions. Table 2.1 indicates that in 1981 in Bahrain, for example, 50 percent of cabinet posts, including the premiership, were held by members of the ruling family.

Third, of the six family-ruled states, two have no written constitutions (Saudi Arabia and Oman), two have provisional constitutions (the United Arab Emirates and Qatar), and only the remaining two (Kuwait and Bahrain) have operated under a written constitution. Although the four written constitutions describe the new process of government as being "democratic," one must be careful not to compare this to any specific form of liberal, democratic government in the West. The "democratization" process in the gulf has primarily been one of transformation from classical tribalism into an urban and affluent form of tribalism.

TABLE 2.1

Council of Ministers: Bahrain (1981)

Minister	Name
Ruler	Shaikh Isa bin Sulman al-Khalifa
Prime minister	Shaikh Khalifa bin Sulman al-Khalifa[a]
Defense	Shaikh Hamad bin Isa al-Khalifa[b]
Foreign affairs	Shaikh Muhammad bin Mubarak al-Khalifa
Interior	Shaikh Muhammad bin Khalifa bin Hamad al-Khalifa
Education	Shaikh 'Abd al-Aziz bin Muhammad al-Khalifa (died in 1981)
Justice and Islamic Affairs	Shaikh 'Abdalla bin Khalid al-Khalifa
Labor and social affairs	Shaikh Isa bin Muhammad al-Khalifa[c]
Finance	Ibrahim 'Abd al-Karim
Development and industry	Yusif Ahmad al-Shirawi
Housing	Shaikh Khalid bin 'Abdullah al-Khalifa
Cabinet affairs	Jawad Salim al-'Urayyid
Legal affairs	Dr. Husayn Muhammad al-Baharna
Health	Dr. Ali Fakhru (moved to Education Ministry in 1982)
Information	Tariq 'Abd al-Rahman al-Muayyid
Public works	Majid al-Jishshi
Transportation	Ibrahim Muhammad Hasan Humaydan
National economy and agriculture	Habib Qasim

[a]Ruler's brother.
[b]Ruler's son.
[c]Replaced in 1981 by Shaikh Khalifa bin Sulman bin Muhammad al-Khalifa.
Source: Compiled by the author.

If one were to examine a case study of political participation in the family-ruled states of the gulf, it would be possible to formulate the following threefold thesis:

1. Evolutionary change in gulf societies, particularly the family-rules amirates, can occur peacefully only through a process of internal political reform. Such a process would involve the establishment of a system that would encourage and guarantee popular participation in the governing of the country.
2. To function effectively and endure peacefully, such participation would have to be institutionalized, both by decree and legislation.
3. While the relationship of the ruler to his people through the daily majlis may be described as "democratic," in contemporary society the people must have a systematic and clearly defined method to reach the ruler and his government and to influence decision making. It will not be long before the "ways of the desert" will be antiquated by the rising level of education of the populace.

The remainder of this chapter will focus on Bahrain's short-lived venture in constitutional government in the mid-1970s. Bahrain offers a useful case study in terms of the nature of the constitutional experiment, the problems it faced, the aspirations of the people involved, the frustrations that ensued, and the relevance of the entire experiment to the gulf as a whole and even to outside parties. In addition, Bahrain is one of those gulf states that became independent in early 1971, along with Qatar, the United Arab Emirates, and Oman. This was less than two years before the eruption of the "energy crisis" on the world scene and the concomitant catapulting of these tiny states into the limelight of international politics.

BAHRAIN'S CONSTITUTIONAL EXPERIENCE:
A BACKGROUND

In his 1971 National Day speech, the first since independence, the amir of Bahrain, Shaikh Isa bin Sulman al-Khalifa, explicitly recognized the need for a constitution. He stated that the constitution would have at least four functions: (a) it would protect the unity and cohesion of the country and of the Bahraini society; (b) it would guarantee the peoples' freedoms of education, work, social welfare, speech, assembly, press, conscience, correspondence, organization, and residence;[2] (c) it would define the citizen's rights and responsibilities in the newly independent state; and (d) it would provide a framework by which the people could participate in the management of their country's affairs in a "context of legitimacy and constitutionalism."[3] The amir's reference to a constitution was the first explicit statement on this issue by a Bahraini official.

Of course, the policy-oriented elites of the Bahraini population responded with enthusiasm to the ruler's address. In a series of long interviews in Bahrain's leading newspaper, al-Adwa', in early 1972, entitled "What Do the People Want in the Constitution?," a clear consensus emerged in support of a constitution.[4] The senior correspondent of al-Adwa', Muhammad Qasim al-Shirawi, presently the paper's editor-in-chief, interviewed representatives of the wealthy merchant class, middle-class businessmen, college graduates, and other members of the country's intelligentsia, and women. A number of those interviewed later became members of the Constitutional Assembly, and some even made it to the National Assembly.

The interviews were published in seven articles: two on merchants; two on the intelligentsia; one on the people as a whole; one on the minister of justice's views; and one on women. The newspaper had intended to interview labor representatives but because of the labor unrest that hit Bahrain in March 1972 and the ensuing sensitive political climate, the interviews were not conducted. Four separate groups emerged from the interviews, each of which articulated its own position and interests. Yet the particularistic interests expressed did not prevent the emergence of a broad consensus. The four groups were: the older and wealthier merchants; the middle-aged and middle-class merchants; the university graduates and the literati; and finally women.

In spite of the different age, socioeconomic position, ideological orientation, and divergent particular interests of those interviewed, a common consensus emerged on the following points: (a) a constitution was needed; (b) popular participation was the popular vehicle for power sharing; (c) a large gap existed between the government (the ruling family) and the people; and (d) this gap is marred with mistrust and suspicion and for the new political system to function effectively and peacefully, this gap must be bridged.[5]

In early May 1972, the ruler invited a number of prominent citizens to the palace for consultations on the nature of the constitution and the structure of the assembly (later came to be called majlis ta'sisi or Constitutional Assembly) that would be established to examine the draft constitution. Several interesting views were expressed during those consultations.[6]

On the constitutional prescription, the following two principles were enunciated by the ruling family: the constitution was to be granted by the amir to his subjects based on the principle of shura; the constitution was neither a response to popular demand nor an extension of popular sovereignty. In a tribal system, authority and legitimacy belonged to the main tribe or the ruling family. Without delving into the value and efficacy of the shura principle, it is sufficient to note that in the Bahraini urban tribal political system, shura continues to undergird the legitimacy to rule. It was understood that power would continue to flow from the apex of the pyramid, which was occupied by the inner councils of the al-Khalifa family.

Three major suggestions developed during the consultations regarding the composition of the Constitutional Assembly: it would consist of government-appointed members; it would be totally elected; and half of it would be elected and the other half appointed. The third suggestion was later adopted.

THE CONSTITUTIONAL ASSEMBLY

On June 20, 1972, the amir promulgated Law No. 12 creating a Constitutional Assembly.[7] According to this law, the assembly would consist of 22 members elected at large by secret ballot, a maximum of 10 members appointed by the amir, and 12 ministers. However, since only 8 were appointed by the amir, the final membership of the Constitutional Assembly was 42.

Once the ruling family, particularly the old guard, and the country as a whole got used to the idea of the impending elections, the mechanics of the election process developed without much difficulty. The country was divided into eight major districts consisting of 19 wards, polling places were set up, and voting registration forms were distributed. Fifty-seven candidates ran on a variety of ideological platforms, and on December 1, 1972 about 27,000 Bahraini male citizens went to the polls to participate in Bahrain's first election. The only act during the election campaign that attracted local and regional attention was the decision of the "leftist bloc" to boycott the election, which was a decision that the bloc later regretted. Also, women were not given suffrage in that election, even though most women's clubs advocated suffrage for women.

To the surprise of many people, the election was held in an atmosphere of freedom. During the few months preceding the election, however, several politically active Bahrainis were arrested for "security" reasons, and some labor strikes occurred in the country. The press was also partially curtailed.

In reviewing the election, one is prompted to make several observations: (a) in spite of the leftists' boycott of the election, a large voter turnout occurred (88.5 percent); (b) many of the elected candidates exhibited similar ideological tendencies (conservative and status quo oriented) to those held by the al-Khalifa leaders; (c) both the campaign and the election results revealed a high degree of religious or sectarian polarization (Shi'a vs. Sunni); (d) in a number of major wards, votes were cast on a sectarian basis, particularly among the Shi'as, and within the heavily Shi'a areas, the vote went to the most conservative candidate, usually a mulla; and finally, (e) the candidates correctly mirrored the male population of the country (see Table 2.2).

As the Constitutional Assembly began its deliberations of the draft constitution, which was prepared by the government, several groupings emerged in the assembly: (a) the ministers, who generally voted as a bloc; (b) the appointed members, a majority of whom were prosperous merchants and businessmen, who mostly did not take an active role in the deliberations but generally supported the government's position; (c) the religious conservative group representing rural districts, which viewed the entire constitutional debate from a fundamentalist Shi'a perspective, thereby strongly defending the Islamic nature of Bahrain and strongly opposing granting women the right to vote; and (d) a loose coalition of liberal, pragmatic, bourgeoisie nationalists, which was rarely able to present a unified position, thereby rendering itself incapable of having any of its major provisions pass in Constitutional Assembly (a member of this group once lamented that it was easier to defeat an article in the draft constitution than to amend it!).

The Constitutional Assembly met roughly twice a week from December 16, 1972 to June 9, 1973, for a total of 45 sessions. Of those meetings, 38 sessions were public and 8 were executive sessions. (The author attended all of the public sessions of the Constitutional Assembly.) The executive sessions dealt with such topics as the bylaws of the assembly, the Islamic nature of the state, and the amir's personal income.

At the conclusion of these sessions and after very interesting and often lively debates that totaled over 150 hours, the Constitutional Assembly approved a draft constitution consisting of 109 articles and presented it to the amir for ratification and promulgation, which was done December 6, 1973. The Constitution consisted of five major chapters: the state; basic principles of society; general rights and duties; branches (the amir, the legislative, the executive, and the judiciary); and general rules and procedures.

The Constitution called for the creation of a National Assembly whose members were to be elected directly by the people by secret ballot. The ministers were also ex officio members of the National Assembly. The assembly was to be, under the amir, the sole legislative body in the country. Article 65 gives the amir the right to dissolve the National Assembly by decree (as long as valid reasons

TABLE 2.2

Elected Constitutional Assembly Members
in Bahrain (December 1972)

Ward	Candidate[a]	Age[b]	Sect	Education	Profession
1	al-Jishshi	38	Shi'a	B.S.	Pharmacist
	al-'Urayyid	50	Shi'a	Elementary	Teacher
2	'Alaywat	43	Shi'a	High School	Merchant
	al-Mahuzi	32	Shi'a	High School	Druggist
3	Kamal al-Din	31	Shi'a	B.A.	Teacher
4	Fakhru	46	Sunni	B.A.	Accountant
5	al-Salih	30	Shi'a	B.A.	Merchant
6	al-'Al	49	Shi'a	High School	Contractor
7	Murad	41	Sunni	High School	Merchant
8	Shamlan	61	Sunni	2 years of college	Merchant
9	Sayyar	44	Sunni	High School	Journalist
	al-Manna'i	36	Sunni	High School	Merchant
10	al-Bin'ali	33	Sunni	B.A.	Lawyer
11	al-Samajihi	31	Shi'a	3 years of college	Teacher
12	Zayn al-Din	42	Shi'a	Religious training	Mulla
13	al-Madani	39	Shi'a	B.A.	Teacher
14	Qasim	32	Shi'a	B.A.	Mulla
15	al-Dayf	53	Shi'a	Religious training	Businessman
16	al-Rashid	35	Sunni	B.A., LLB	Lawyer
17	al-'Ali	40	Shi'a	Elementary	Contractor
18	al-Mutawwaj	38	Shi'a	High School	Merchant
19	al-Fadil	47	Sunni	High School	Merchant

[a]Family name.
[b]Minimum age requirements for candidacy is 30.
<u>Source</u>: Compiled by the author.

are given. However, according to Section 2 of the same article, if the National Assembly is dissolved, elections for a new assembly should be held on later than two months from the date of dissolution. If no such elections are held (Section 3), the dissolved assembly will regain all of its constitutional authority and will convene as if it had not been dissolved.

The debate in the Constitutional Assembly focused on three major constitutional questions: legitimacy, popular participation, and power sharing among the branches of government. Looking at the draft constitution that finally emerged from the assembly, one can safely state that it was a document that correctly reflected the Bahraini state and the mainstream of Bahraini society. Consider what the Constitution says on the three areas mentioned above.

Concerning legitimacy, the Bahraini Constitution establishes several principles: (a) "Bahrain is a sovereign independent Islamic Arab state" (Article 1, Section A); (b) "Bahrain's rule is hereditary, vested in the person and descendants of Shaikh Isa bin Sulman al-Khalifa, from father to eldest son" (Article 1, Section B); (c) "Islam is the official religion of the state, and Islamic law (Shari'a) is a primary source of legislation" (Article 2); and (d) "the Amir is the head of state, and his person is protected and above reproach" (Article 33).

Concerning popular participation, the following principles are established: "the system of government in Bahrain is democratic and the people are the source of authority" (Article 1, Section D); "thirty members of the National Assembly are to be popularly elected by secret ballot according to the provisions of the Elections Law" (Article 43, Section A); the freedoms of conscience, speech, press, correspondence, and organization are protected by law (Articles 22, 23, 24, 26, and 27); and "members of the National Assembly represent the whole people" (Article 63, Section A).

The Bahraini Constitution theoretically establishes three branches of government: a legislative branch, an executive branch, and a judicial branch. However, in practice, the picture is less clear. Not only is the amirship established as an autonomous branch that overrides the other three, but also the ministers sit in the National Assembly as members ex officio, with a vote (Article 43, Section B). Unlike the separation of powers in Western democracies, the legislative branch in Bahrain is headed jointly by the amir and the National Assembly (Article 32, Sections A and B). The amir also "heads the executive branch jointly with the Council of Ministers, and judicial decisions are rendered in his name" (Article 32, Section B). Furthermore, "laws become effective only when approved by the National Assembly and ratified by the Amir" (Article 42). The judiciary, however, seems to be more independent than the other two branches. "The judiciary is independent and autonomous, and no interference is permitted in the administration of justice" (Article 101, Section B).

THE NATIONAL ASSEMBLY

In accordance with the Constitution, over 29,000 Bahraini male citizens went to the polls on December 7, 1973 to elect Bahrain's first National Assembly. That election had special significance because of the timing, the national and regional context, and some unexpected voting patterns that emerged. Bahrain was the first of the lower gulf Arab states to have a constitution, a popular election, and a representative body. In fact, of all the gulf Arab states, only Bahrain and Kuwait even attempted to operate under a functional constitution of any kind.

More importantly, Bahrain's National Assembly election was the first such election in any gulf or Arab country after the October War. Secondly, the election was held within the context of the oil embargo with which the gulf Arab states levered themselves into the center of international politics. The singularity of the election was further enhanced when one considered the strong participation of Bahrain's leftist forces in the election and the seemingly surprising victory of at least eight candidates from that bloc. Another interesting aspect of this first encounter with democracy was the relatively open atmosphere surrounding the election. The al-Khalifa ruling family decided to allow a free atmosphere to prevail during the period immediately preceding the election; the people responded by overwhelmingly electing candidates from the leftist/nationalist/reformist bloc.

Like the Constitutional Assembly election a year earlier, the National Assembly election went very smoothly, albeit with much more excitement. Of the 112 candidates who ran in the country's 20 wards, 30 were elected. Over 30 percent of the elected members of the Constitutional Assembly were reelected to the National Assembly. The National Assembly was perhaps more representative of the country as a whole than the Constitutional Assembly, which was largely due to the participation of the labor-supported reform-oriented ("leftist") bloc in the election. Like the Constitutional Assembly, the National Assembly election did not have women voters. Also the National Assembly membership included intelligentsia, bourgeoisie nationalists, reformists, conservative mullas, and of course businessmen (see Table 2.3).

The first National Assembly was first convened by the amir under the Constitution on December 16, 1973. That legislative

TABLE 2.3

Elected National Assembly Members in Bahrain (December 1973)

Ward	Candidate[a]	Age[b]	Sect	Education	Profession
1	al-Jishshi	39	Shi'a	B.S.	Pharmacist
	al-Dhawadi[c]	34	Sunni	M.S.	Attorney
2	Khalaf[c],[d]	30	Shi'a	Ph.D.	Professor
	al-Jishshi	49	Shi'a	High School	High School Principal
3	Hammad[c]	31	Sunni	Licentiate in Law	Attorney
4	Hirmis	32	Sunni	High School	Merchant
	Marhun[c]	31	Sunni	M.S.	Attorney
5	al-Salih	32	Shi'a	B.A.	Merchant
6	'Ubul[c]	33	Sunni	B.A.	Businessman
7	al-'Al	51	Shi'a	High School	Contractor
8	Murad	42	Sunni	High School	Businessman
	al-Ma'awda[c]	30	Shi'a	High School	Civil Servant
9	Rabi'a[c]	33	Sunni	High School	Car Insurance Executive
	Sabah[c]	42	Sunni	High School	Businessman
10	al-Dhawadi[c]	30	Sunni	High School	Employee in business
	Fakhru	58	Sunni	Self-educated	Merchant
11	al-Bin'ali	34	Sunni	B.A.	Attorney
12	'Ali	31	Shi'a	G.C.E.	Accountant
13	al'Qassab	39	Shi'a	High School	Teacher
	al-Sharkhat	38	Shi'a	High School	Employee at Bapco
14	al-Madani	40	Shi'a	Religious training	Teacher
15	Qasim	33	Shi'a	Religious training	Editor and Mulla
	al-Jamri	35	Shi'a	Religious training	Mulla
16	'Ali	35	Shi'a	Religious training	Mulla
17	Kamal	40	Sunni	High School	Businessman
18	al-'Ali	42	Shi'a	Elementary	Contractor
19	al-Mutawwaj	40	Shi'a	High School	Merchant
	Nasir	50	Shi'a	High School	Teacher
20	al-Khalifa	31	Sunni	High School	N.A.[e]
	al-Dhahrani	31	Sunni	Vocational School	Civil Servant

[a]Family name.

[b]Minimum age requirement for candidacy is 30.

[c]Member of the reform-oriented ("leftist") bloc.

[d]He was disqualified later because of misrepresentation of age.

[e]Not available.

Source: State of Bahrain, Ministry of Information, Akhbar al-Bahrain (December 10, 1973), pp. 3-7.

session ended June 30, 1974, after 54 meetings, mostly on Wednesdays and Sundays. The session was not exceptionally eventful; several meetings were spent on procedural matters pertaining to the bylaws of the assembly. The second and last legislative session of the National Assembly was held October 23, 1974 and lasted for approximately 50 meetings until June 1975. During that legislative session, particularly in early 1975, many meetings were characterized by rancor and open hostility between the government/ruling family and some members, especially those belonging to the leftist-reformist bloc. Rational debate turned into hostile confrontations; attitudes hardened and ideological positions polarized. Among the major issues that occupied the National Assembly in late spring 1975 were inflation, high prices, housing, the national budget, government expenditures, internal security, gulf security, and the U.S. naval presence at the facility at Jufair, just outside Manama.

The processes of the National Assembly virtually came to a halt by May 1975. Accusations and allegations prevailed. The government claimed that the leftists, or "communists" as the government called them, in the National Assembly were intent on destroying the entire democratic experiment; this bloc in turn claimed the government, particularly the prime minister, was no longer interested in continuing the democratic experiment and was determined to undermine the entire process of popular participation. It was also alleged, particularly by leftist elements in the National Assembly, that the ruling family was under foreign pressure (from Saudi Arabia, Iran, and the United States) to end the whole experiment. They also alleged that the public security bill that was sponsored by the government and was the focus of heated debate in the assembly was an indication that the ruling family was seriously considering the curtailment of the freedom of expression, which was the cornerstone of the democratic experiment. The government replied that only the Communist elements were targeted.

The confrontation between the government and the National Assembly led the government to boycott the last few sessions of the assembly. The prime minister maintained that it was impossible for him or for his ministers to work with the assembly. Accordingly, he submitted his resignation to his brother the amir and proposed that the National Assembly be dissolved and be restructured under a new election law. [8] The amir accepted the government's resignation and asked the prime minister to form a new government. On August 26, 1975, the amir dissolved the National Assembly (Decree No. 14, 1975) under Article 65, Section 1 of the Constitution. At the same time, he ordered (Order No. 4, 1975) that Section 2 of the same article, which called for a new election within two months, be suspended. [9] Thus the entire democratic experiment in Bahrain came to an end.

RECENT DEVELOPMENTS

Since the dissolution of the National Assembly, the Council of Ministers has performed both the executive as well as the legislative functions. Since 1975 laws and other official decrees have been issued in the name of the Constitution, but without a parliament. Unlike the situation in Kuwait, where the dissolution of the Kuwaiti National Assembly was accompanied by an amiri promise that parliamentary elections would be held within four years, no such amiri statement was issued in Bahrain. The government's legal experts have consistently argued that the dissolution of the National Assembly did not mean that the entire Constitution was disregarded. On the contrary, Dr. Hussein al-Baharna, minister of state for legal affairs, in a recent newspaper interview, argued that Bahrain was still committed to the Constitution.[10]

In the same interview, Dr. al-Baharna stated that the dissolution of the National Assembly basically involved the transfer of the legislative function from the assembly to the Council of Ministers. Secondly, although some articles in the Constitution have been suspended, he has maintained that the Constitution as a whole is still intact. He further stated that Bahraini officials are anxious to resurrect the parliamentary experiment in Bahrain.

Several other statements have been made in the last two years by other Bahraini leaders about the possible return of parliamentary life to the country. Other gulf leaders have also voiced similar opinions. It is safe to assume that this flurry of statements about popular participation has been caused by the Iranian revolution and the fall of the Shah. What happened in Iran was an indication to many gulf ruling families that military force cannot keep a ruler in power if a popular antiregime movement spreads throughout the country.

Secondly, as was pointed out, members of the ruling families are now convinced that regional stability and security are inexorably linked to domestic stability. In this context, internal stability means the establishment of a functional system of power sharing in which the people participate more or less in the governing of the country on a regular institutionalized basis.

Early in 1980, Kuwait, Bahrain, and Saudi Arabia sent out clear signals that it was only a matter of time before popular participation is established.

In late February 1980, Prince Fahd of Saudi Arabia revealed that a ministerial committee was to be established for the purpose of drafting a constitution or "a basic system of government" as the Saudis call it. Indeed, an eight-member ministerial committee was set up a month later for this purpose.[11] No results have been revealed to date.

On February 10, 1980, the amir of Kuwait, Shaikh Jabir al-Ahmad al-Jabir al-Sabah, issued an Amiri Decree setting up a national committee to revise Kuwait's constitution.[12] The Constitution was first promulgated in 1962 and was partially suspended in August 1976 when the late amir, Shaikh Sabah al-Ahmad al-Sabah dissolved the National Assembly.

The 35-member committee for the revision of the Constitution was charged with the responsibility of submitting a report to the Council of Ministers detailing the constitutional articles that, in the committee's judgment, should be amended and the reasons for the proposed amendments. In establishing the committee, the Amiri Decree authorized ministers to attend the committee sessions but without a vote. Although there has been no official announcement of the names of the committee members, it was believed that of the 35 members, 11 are former members of the dissolved National Assembly. As a result of the work of the committee and with the full support of the ruling family, a new National Assembly was elected in Kuwait in February 1981, thereby reviving the parliamentary life in the country, which had been suspended since August 1976.

In an interview with al-Qabas newspaper (Kuwait) in April 1980, Bahrain's foreign minister, Shaikh Muhammad bin Mubarak al-Khalifa, revealed that the question of democracy has been widely discussed within Bahrain's ruling family. He declared that the government was "seriously studying the formulation of a practical, realistic and acceptable plan for a return to parliamentary life."[13] While expressing the hope that the National Assembly would be reinstituted by the end of the year, the foreign minister indicated that consultations between Bahrain, Kuwait, and Saudi Arabia on this question are being held regularly.

In reviving the parliamentary system, Shaikh Muhammad bin Mubarak said that three basic considerations must be understood:

1. It would be a mistake to think that Arab gulf states are seeking to establish an "ideal" system of democracy. Instead, what is being sought is a system that would reflect the present conditions and realities of the region.

2. The forms of popular representation that gulf governments intend to adopt in the different states should be close to each other (mutaqaribah) but not exactly similar (mutatabiqah). Even though the countries have many common characteristics, their individual experiences have varied significantly.

3. Democracy and popular participation in government are two basic requirements at this juncture of Arab gulf history, and they are directly linked to internal stability. The government of

Bahrain, according to Shaikh Muhammad, is genuinely convinced of this linkage and is seriously seeking to implement a democratic system of government.

The foreign minister's analysis of the present situation in Bahrain and of long-term stability in the gulf is extremely revealing. As a prominent gulf leader, his views will undoubtedly shape the parliamentary system that might emerge in Bahrain, as well as in other gulf amirates.

However, it would be naive to ignore the direct impact that the Islamic revolution in Iran has had on the Arab side of the gulf, particularly in forcing the Arab rulers to reconsider their relationship with their peoples. The fact is that the popular revolution and the collapse of the Pahlavi dynasty have been very traumatic for the ruling families throughout the gulf region. That an Islamic regime came to power in Iran and that Islam is also the predominant religion in neighboring Arab states has not been comforting to such a staunchly religious state as Saudi Arabia.

The revolution in Iran has signaled neighboring states that their internal security is problematical. As mentioned earlier, it is always possible that internal dissent in neighboring countries might some day, perhaps in the not-too-distant future, erupt into violence, which in turn might threaten the existence of the familial regimes on the Arab side of the gulf. If this situation occurs, it is obvious that not only the Arab societies will be disturbed; the interests of many outside powers that rely on gulf oil will also be strongly affected.

Al-Qabas newspaper also interviewed other al-Khalifa ministers and some former members of the National Assembly. The interviews revealed the existence of three different positions within the ruling family on the revival of parliamentary life in Bahrain. Some ministers have advocated that all members hould be elected, others have argued for a combined formula of election and appointments, and still others have called for an appointed National Assembly, at least at the initial stage.[14] It is of course difficult to predict what form of National Assembly will emerge, but even though the foreign minister's prediction has not yet come true, it is safe to say that some sort of parliament will be reinstituted.

The opinions expressed by former members of the National Assembly in these interviews revealed that three general ideological groups exist in Bahrain: the centrists, consisting of the bourgeois nationalist middle class and upper middle class; the leftists, consisting of the reform-oriented intelligentsia and professionals; and the religious, consisting mostly of conservative rural Shi'a mullas. Predictably, the three groups have espoused different views on the

composition of the posited National Assembly.[15] A leading spokes-
man for the centrist bloc, Jasim Murad, a prosperous businessman
and active civic leader, has indicated recently that he would favor a
National Assembly with two-thirds of its members elected and one-
third appointed by the amir.[16] The leftist bloc, according to one of
their prominent spokesmen, 'Ali Rabi'a, have argued for a totally
elected assembly. The religious bloc has adopted a surprisingly low
profile on this whole question. It could be that this wait-and-see
attitude stems from the fact that most of the religious mullas are
Shi'as and hence are somewhat more sensitive toward the Sunni al-
Khalifa ruling family.

The "great debate" on the resumption of parliamentary life
in Bahrain has continued into 1981, with more statements and ex-
planations. Three spokesmen have dominated the debate: Shaikh
Muhammad bin Mubarak representing the moderate view within the
ruling family; Jasim Murad representing the middle-class liberal
bourgeoisie view; and 'Ali Rabi'a representing the reformist/leftist
view.[17] Editorials have also appeared in some of the gulf's most
widely read newspapers advocating a return to "democracy" in
Bahrain and in other gulf states.[18] The debate continues with
Shaikh Muhammad maintaining that parliamentary life would return
once a proper formula is developed.[19] The foreign minister seems
to express the belief that "political participation is the basis of rule,
and that the ruling family has accepted this view. It is only a
matter of time."[20]

REFLECTIONS

In reviewing the parliamentary experiment in Bahrain and as
a result of extensive interviews of most of the participants in the
process, it is possible to make the following observations on the
suspension of the process less than two years after it had begun:

1. Becoming a democratic nation required more than just an
intent on the part of the ruler and the ruling family to "open up" the
regime.

2. Participatory government and continued centralized family
rule seem to be contradictory. Sharing in government requires
both rights and responsibilities as well as a sincere commitment to
the spirit of compromise.

3. Because of education, communications, and, above all,
the oil wealth, the ruling families could not keep foreign ideas from
invading their societies. Consequently, the traditional family-type
communal relationship between the ruler and his people began to

face tremendous social strains. Traditionalism needed to yield to new social demands.

4. The whole constitutional experiment seems to have started off incorrectly. The rhetoric of democracy could not measure up to the reality of centralized government and, when a conflict erupted between the people and the ruling family over the source of authority, the so-called "game of democracy" came to a halt, with individual liberty on the losing end.

5. Perhaps the whole attempt to become democratic was premature. A successful democratic process requires more than instant wealth to translate the people's goodwill and traditional loyalty and support into a functional system of participatory government. What might be needed first is a commitment to create a more rational economy in those societies.

6. For democracy to function effectively at least three basic conditions must be fulfilled: the relationship between the government and the governed must be clearly defined; democracy must be recognized as a right that belongs to the people, rather than being a gift from the ruler; and the process must become institutionalized and not subject to the whim of any one ruler or ruling family. These conditions were absent.

7. Other factors aiding the establishment and functioning of a democratic system are: a reasonable level of education and literacy, a healthy economy, a reasonably large middle class, a fairly self-reliant indigenous population and, of course, an effective government based on a tradition of voluntary compliance with the law. These elements were only partially present.

On the positive side, in reviewing recent statements from Bahrain, one can be cautiously optimistic about the prospects of some form of parliamentary life in the country. Some gulf ruling families have come to accept the view that if channeled properly, popular participation can be an asset to the regime and a stabilizing force in society. In this case "democracy" is not only good for the moral sensibilities of libertarians; it is also good in the long run for the continued survival of the regimes.

For the democratization process to succeed, steps toward political participation must be taken carefully and gradually. Like other gulf amirates, Bahrain is a newly independent state, with a budding political system. Because of their prominence in international economics and politics, due of course to oil, these states often tend to receive intense international scrutiny.

Furthermore, the absence of participatory government in these states is not unique to the gulf; democratic government is lacking in most Arab countries that have been independent for several decades. One can empathize with Bahrain's foreign minister when he recently questioned the unrelenting focus on democracy in the gulf and not in the rest of the Arab world.

Finally, a genuine commitment exists among many elites for "opening up" the regime and for inviting some type of responsible popular participation in government. This conclusion is based on the author's own field research and observations in Bahrain, on his attendance of all the public sessions of the Constitutional Assembly, on reading all of the minutes of Bahrain's National Assembly, and on talking to many Bahrainis over the years. Democracy or popular participation can take many different forms, and as long as the process is based on the realities and cultural heritage of the country, one can be hopeful that some goodwill come out of the enterprise.

Bahrain's experience with popular participation is a microcosm of the difficulties all of these states face in resolving questions of political legitimacy. Although they have devised different solutions, the common assumption is that popular participation is necessary to ensure political stability. As mentioned in the beginning of this chapter, political stability is a necessary but not sufficient factor in regional security. Other important factors impinging on this security are the Palestine conflict, regional cooperation, and U.S. policy. These issues will be examined in subsequent chapters.

NOTES

1. The Middle East (London), June, July, August, September 1980.

2. Later adopted as articles 22, 23, 24, 25, 26, 27, and 28 in the Bahraini Constitution. State of Bahrain, Constitution of the State of Bahrain (December 6, 1973). A supplement to al-Jarida al-Rasmiyya [Official Gazette], no. 1049.

3. State of Bahrain, Ministry of Information, Huna al-Bahrain (December 1971), p. 3; Emile A. Nakhleh, Bahrain: Political Development in a Modernizing Society (Lexington, Mass.: D. C. Heath, 1976), pp. 117-64.

4. Al-Adwa' (Bahrain), February-April 1972.

5. Nakhleh, Bahrain, p. 118.

6. Sada al-'Usbu' (Bahrain), May 23, 30, 1972. Also based on the author's interviews with some of those present at the meetings.

7. State of Bahrain, Official Gazette, June 20, 1972, pp. 3-8.

8. al-Adwa' (Bahrain), August 28, 1975, p. 2.

9. Ibid., p. 3.

10. Ibid., January 24, 1981, p. 3.

11. Washington Post, March 2, 1980; FBIS 5 (March 25, 1980:C3-4.

12. Middle East Economic Survey 23 (February 18, 1980):4-5.

13. al-Qabas (Kuwait), April 12, 1980, p. 10. See also al-Mustaqbal (Paris), July 12, 1980, pp. 28-29.

14. al-Qabas (Kuwait), April 13, 1980, p. 9.

15. Ibid., April 14, 1980, p. 11. See also an interview with other former members of the National Assembly in al-Masirah (Bahrain), July 17, 1980, pp. 8-9; July 24, 1980, pp. 4-6; August 7, 1980, pp. 4-6.

16. al-Adwa' (Bahrain), April 12, 1980, p. 5; Akhbar al-Khaleej (Bahrain), February 7, 1980, p. 7.

17. al-Qabas (Kuwait), April 19, 20, 1981.

18. al-Adwa' (Bahrain), January 10, 1981, p. 3; al-Khaleej (Dubai), January 31, 1981, p. 1.

19. al-Adwa' (Bahrain), January 17, 1981, p. 1.

20. Ibid.

3

GULF COOPERATION
AND REGIONAL SECURITY

INTRODUCTION

Cooperation among Persian Gulf states since the early 1970s has taken different forms and has existed on several levels: economic, cultural, educational, informational, technical, commercial, and military. The rhetoric of cooperation has often exceeded the reality, but gulf states have embarked on a series of cooperative arrangements in all of these fields.

At least four levels of cooperation among these states can be delineated: bilateral, multilateral or regional, OAPEC, and Arab League. Other forms of cooperation have been generated through international (United Nations-related) agencies such as the International Monetary Fund, the United Nations Development Program, the International Labor Organization, the World Health Organization, and the United Nations Educational Scientific and Cultural Organization.

Again, the nature of cooperation has varied depending on the issue and the country or countries involved. An example of a successful bilateral cooperative project is the Kuwaiti-Bahraini agreement on education and health under which Kuwait has funded the construction and maintenance of schools and hospitals in Bahrain. Other examples include the Saudi-Bahraini agreement to build a causeway connecting the two countries, with Saudi Arabia financing the bulk of the project; and the Saudi-Bahraini agreement over the Saudi Abu Sa'fa offshore oil field in which Bahrain receives half of its revenues.

An example of a successful regional cooperative project is the Arab Shipbuilding and Repair Yard Company (ASRY) in Bahrain. It is one of the few ship repair yards in the world designed to handle super oil tankers. ASRY is owned by the seven OAPEC countries: Bahrain, Iraq, Kuwait, Libya, Qatar, Saudi Arabia, and the United Arab Emirates. Since it began its operations in September 1977, ASRY has shown an impressive record of success.[1]

Among the other joint-government-owned projects, in addition to ASRY, are the Arab Maritime Petroleum Transport Company, the Arab Petroleum Investments Company, and the Arab Petroleum Services Company.

Of course, cooperation has been far more prevalent among the Arab states than between the Arab states and Iran. Even among the Arab states, more cooperation has occurred among the states of the lower gulf than between these states and Iraq.

Several factors have pushed gulf states toward cooperation: a feeling of insecurity, particularly in the late 1960s and early 1970s, due to their small size; an anxiety regarding the ambitions of outside powers regarding the gulf; the "energy crisis" and the rising dependence of the industrial world on gulf oil; the internal threats of leftist and radical movements against the tribal regimes of many gulf states; the small size of the indigenous populations with the corresponding shortage of local trained personnel and the concomitant influx of expatriate labor; the Iranian threat perceived by some gulf states, both during the Shah's reign and under the Knomeini regime; and finally, the realization on the part of some states that cooperation is in their best national interest. In sum, the practicalities of survival as independent political units have contributed to making cooperation a reality.

One of the early joint ventures dealt with the creation of a regional airline with related services. This project has expanded to include: an airline (Gulf Air) owned by four states; a civil aviation college in Qatar; joint airline arrangements with the Saudi, Kuwaiti, North Yemeni, and Sudanese airlines.[2]

A list of joint projects involving the gulf states follows. These projects were sponsored by the Arab League, the Arab Economic Unity Council, individual governments, two or more governments, or by OAPEC.

Arab Economic Unity Council (1964), which was founded to establish
    and oversee other projects.
Arab Common Market (1965).
Industrial Development Center for Arab States (1969).
Arab Organization for Industrialization (1975).
Arab Federation for Chemical Fertilizers (1974).
Arab Monetary Fund (1975).
Arab Company for Agriculture and Food Production (1975).

Arab Organization for Mineral Resources (1977).
Kuwait Fund for Arab Economic Development (1974).
Abu Dhabi Fund for Arab Economic Development (1971).
Saudi Development Fund (1974).
Arab Fund for Economic and Social Development (1971).
Islamic Development Fund (1974).
Arab Investment Company (1974).
Gulf International Bank (1975).
Gulf Arab News Agency (1977).
Gulf Arab University (1980).
Gulf Cooperation Council (1981).[3]

In order to place the above list of cooperative projects in proper perspective, two comments are necessary. First, although the seeds of cooperation among gulf states have been planted, economic competition among these states has yet to yield cooperation. ASRY is one example. Following OAPEC's approval of the project and after the work had already started in Bahrain, Dubai, a member amirate of the United Arab Emirates, proceeded on its own to build another dry dock in Dubai. This has also occurred with petrochemical plants, airports, and even colleges and universities.

Second, parochial images of national prestige continue to dominate the regional collective interests of the states involved. Economic common sense dictates that shortages of trained manpower, limited markets, high prices, and duplication of efforts and costs should produce coordination in planning and execution of projects. However, this has not yet happened. For example, there has been little, if any, exchange of information among gulf states regarding industrialization plans.

However, the creation of the Gulf Cooperation Council (GCC) in 1981 seems to indicate a positive change of attitude toward cooperation. It is an ambitious project that has already raised many hopes and expectations among gulf leaders and elites.

THE GULF COOPERATION COUNCIL

Recognizing that their region is coveted by outside powers for economic and strategic reasons and further recognizing that they must not only survive but be able to influence events in their midst, leaders of six gulf Arab countries—Saudi Arabia, Kuwait, Bahrain, Qatar, the United Arab Emirates, and Oman—decided in the spring of 1981 to form the GCC. Although the desire for unity and close cooperation has been present for several years, as witnessed in official statements of the leaders of those states over the years,

events in the last three years have compelled these leaders to hasten
the pace of cooperation. Some of these events, of course, include
the fall of the Shah, the continued chaos in Iran, the Sunni-Shi'a religious conflict (with the Khomeini regime spearheading Shi'ism as
an aggressive force against tribal Sunni Arab regimes across the
gulf), and the Soviet invasion of Afghanistan. The Iraq-Iran war,
while currently restricted to the upper tip of the gulf, remains a
source of anxiety to the rest of the gulf states.

Whatever the catalyst, the six gulf states decided in May 1981
to establish the GCC, which was ratified by the heads of those states
in Abu Dhabi on May 26, 1981.[4]

The treaty setting up the GCC consists of a preamble and 19
articles. The basic purposes of the GCC are specified in Article 4:

    1. To achieve coordination and cooperation among
the member states in all fields as a prelude for unity.

    2. To strengthen the ties, contacts, and facets of
cooperation among the peoples of the member states in
different fields.

    3. To establish similar procedures and practices
among the member states in the following fields:

        a. finance and economics;
        b. commerce, customs, and communications;
        c. education and culture;
        d. social welfare and health;
        e. information and tourism; and
        f. legislation and public administration.

    4. To support scientific and technological prog-
ress in the fields of industry, mining, agriculture,
marine and animal resources, to establish scientific
research centers and common projects, and to encourage the cooperation of the private sector for the
good of the peoples of the member countries.

According to the treaty, the GCC will have its headquarters
in Riyadh, Saudi Arabia (Article 2) and will operate on the basis of
a one-state one-vote rule. Unanimity is required on substantive issues and a majority on procedural issues. The structure of the
GCC includes four major organs: a Supreme Council consisting of
the heads of the member states (Articles 6-9); an Arbitration Commission (Articles 6 and 10); a Ministerial Council consisting of the
foreign ministers of the member states (Articles 6 and 11-14); and
a Secretariat (Articles 6, 14, and 15).

A brief synopsis of the articles in the GCC treaty follows:

The preamble of the GCC indicates that underlying this agreement were shared common bonds, special relations, common characteristics, similar regimes, a common religion (Islam), and a common destiny. As is apparent in the statements of government officials following the signing of the agreement, another major purpose of the new council is to coordinate regional security matters among the member states, ranging from exchanging security information to a common defense strategy.

Immediately following the signing of the GCC treaty, the convening heads of state approved a "Working Paper for Joint Gulf Action" under the auspices of the GCC. Five standing committees were established under the "Working Paper": (1) Social and Economic Planning Committee; (2) Commercial, Economic, and Financial Cooperation Committee; (3) Industrial Cooperation Committee; (4) Oil Committee; and (5) Cultural Services Committee.

In addition, the "Working Paper" made the following three points:

The establishment of the GCC is a response to the historic, geographic, economic, cultural, political, and strategic realities of the Persian Gulf.

The move to establish a larger entity for gulf states is designed to protect the stability, security, and progress of the region.

The GCC shall attempt to provide the peoples of the region with real and continuous growth, while at the same time it shall strive to protect peace, security, and progress. The basic issue is how to transform the oil-generated wealth into comprehensive and steady growth for the welfare of the people of the region. [5]

It is, of course, still too early to assess the success of the GCC in the social, economic, and political areas, but there has been a noticeable tendency to cooperate in the field of internal security. The antiregime conspiracy that was uncovered in Bahrain in mid-December 1981 generated a quick and active response from the member states of the GCC. This response came initially in the form of statements of support for the al-Khalifa family of Bahrain from neighboring states but was followed by mutual security agreements proposed by Saudi Arabia.

Indeed, immediately in the aftermath of the Bahraini plot, the Saudi interior minister, Price Nayef ibn 'Abd al-'Aziz, visited several neighboring states and strongly encouraged them to endorse the Saudi strategy of gulf security based on a system of bilateral security treaties. This approach seems to coincide with some official statements made immediately following the founding of the GCC. One representative statement was made by Bahrain's foreign minister, Shaikh Muhammad bin Mubarak al-Khalifa. In a newspaper interview, the foreign minister stated that the GCC was created as a response to the enormous challenges facing the gulf—economically, politically, socially, and even strategically. [6] This is an era of large units in international relations, rather than small states, he said, and in the absence of political unification, the GCC model of cooperation and coordination affords a better position. The foreign minister made two other points. First, "the GCC is not an alliance against anyone, nor does it harbor any aggressive intentions or plans against any party. The GCC calls for regional peace and stability. "[7] Second, the idea of a cooperative arrangement similar to what finally emerged in the GCC agreement has been discussed off and on since the first years of independence in the early 1970s. The two meetings of the foreign ministers of the six states in Riyadh, Saudi Arabia in February 1981 and in Muscat, Oman in March 1981 were only the culmination of previous discussions regarding cooperation. [8]

Beyond economic cooperation on the local level, the GCC is expected to play an international role, particularly in the political/ security areas. This role was discussed at length by the GCC's secretary-general, 'Abdalla Bishara, in a wide-ranging press interview in July 1981. [9] A summary of Bishara's comments follows:

1. Arab unity is the best way to deal not only with Israel, but also with the United States. The way the United States has treated the Arabs is insulting, and the best answer to U.S. policy would be an Arab policy based on solidarity.

2. Gulf states do not believe that Western security assistance would be the best way to ensure the outflow of oil from the gulf. On the contrary, they believe that the U.S. Rapid Deployment Force would directly or indirectly invite the Soviet Union to intervene in the area. Gulf states want no country—the United States, Great Britain, or the Soviet Union—to gain a foothold in this area.

3. The GCC is in favor of "gulfanization" of gulf security; that is, this security should be left to the people of the gulf alone. A threat to the stability and internal security of any GCC member is therefore considered a threat to the stability and internal security of all members.

4. The GCC does not accept the Soviet proposal of an international conference to neutralize the gulf because such a neutralization would be futile while Soviet troops remain in Afghanistan and Soviet naval forces cruise the Indian Ocean and the Arabian Sea with facilities in various Red Sea and Arabian Sea ports. However, it is possible that some time in the future diplomatic relations might be established between the Soviet Union and GCC states.

5. The GCC member states have identical political systems, foreign policies, ideologies, aspirations, and personal, social, and political problems. Some of these problems, according to Bishara, include oil drilling, pricing, and marketing, foreign threats, small indigenous populations, shortages of Arab-trained manpower, and expanding economies. [10] In response to these problems, the GCC has concluded agreements to cover three major areas: the coordination of oil policy (exploration, production, pricing, and marketing); the free movement of gulf nationals among the six member states; and the right to own property in any of the member states by a national of any of the six states regardless of the person's place of birth.

Beyond these official statements, the creation of the Gulf Cooperation Council has been supported by the political leaders of the member states and representatives of the elites in those states. The support of the former group has been strong, particularly in the application of cooperation to gulf security, while elite support has been clear but somewhat cautious. The remainder of this chapter will focus on these two areas.

THE GULF COOPERATION COUNCIL
AND GULF ELITES

In an 11-part series of interviews published in the Kuwaiti newspaper, al-Qabas, in February 1981, the GCC was examined closely by a number of Kuwaiti intellectuals—professors, bureaucrats, and businessmen.[11] Those interviewed supported the creation of the GCC, and they felt that the Gulf Cooperation Council should work toward six specific goals: (1) a better coordinated and more rational economic planning; (2) social justice and more equitable distribution of wealth; (3) popular participation in the governing process; (4) support of the Palestinian people; (5) keeping the gulf outside of superpower rivalry and free of foreign military bases; and (6) paving the way for genuine unity among the peoples of the region and not limiting the envisioned cooperation to the rulers and regimes only.

These interviews, together with other articles throughout 1981, give us a clear picture of the view from within the gulf concerning regional cooperation and its impact on regional security. Accordingly, it would be useful to consider these views and perceptions in more detail.

Dr. Muhammad al-Rumaihi, a sociology professor at the University of Kuwait, stated that although the GCC is a step forward, several provisions in the agreement are vague and require further action.[12] He also said that better financial and economic distribution among the states of the region is necessary. According to Rumaihi, joint action is good, particularly if it serves the interests of the peoples of the region—economically, socially, politically, and strategically. He maintained that the creation of the GCC should strengthen the eastern corner of the Arab world and in turn should contribute to the defense of the entire region.

What is important, according to Professor Rumaihi, is the content rather than the form of cooperation. The framers of this cooperation should keep in mind two essential points: that regional security is linked to internal stability, and that the latter can be guaranteed only through social justice and political participation. Finally, Professor Rumaihi cautioned the member states not to limit cooperation to security issues alone.

In another interview, Dr. Muhammad Rashid al-Fil, professor of geography at the University of Kuwait, elaborated upon the two essential components of security: food and the military.[13] He said that human development and the guaranteeing of food and military security should head the list of priorities of the GCC. Although the basis of gulf cooperation varies significantly from the West European model, according to Dr. al-Fil, regional cooperation should involve the peoples of the different gulf countries. These peoples should be encouraged through popularly elected bodies to interact with each other so that a stronger base of unity would be established.

The GCC is a step toward Arab unity, and it is only a matter of time before Iraq joins the GCC (a similar point was made regarding Iraq's absence by Professor Rumaihi in the previous interview). The people of the gulf belong to one race and speak one language, stated Dr. al-Fil, and they also face common challenges. The two most important of these challenges are a shortage of foodstuffs and a shortage of indigenous trained manpower.

A more positive attitude was expressed in the interview with Isa Majid al-Shahin, secretary-general of the Gulf States Cooperation Committee in the foreign ministry of Kuwait.[14] Al-Shahin perceives the GCC as a response to the belief of the peoples and governments of the region that they alone are responsible for the protection of gulf security, stability, and resources. He also stated that the GCC is capable of meeting the present dangers facing the gulf. Among these dangers are foreign interference, border disputes, expatriate labor, and the absence of popular political participation.

Specific questions were raised about some articles in the GCC treaty in another interview. Dr. Adil al-Tabtaba'i, professor of law at the University of Kuwait, argues that some provisions in the agreement, such as voting, must be clarified.[15] He also stated that since the GCC is perceived as an initial step toward Arab national unity, Iraq should be invited to join the working committee, but not necessarily the Supreme Council. He further recommended that the GCC unify the member states' oil policies, their foreign policies, and their diplomatic representation. Senior-level councils should also be set up under the auspices of the GCC for information, oil, and foreign investment.

A political analysis of the supports and policies of the GCC would indicate, according to Dr. Walid Mubarak, a professor of political science at the University of Kuwait, that comprehensive regional cooperation is necessary for domestic and foreign political considerations.[16] Dr. Mubarak envisioned three possible paths of cooperation within the GCC: political, economic, and social. To succeed in its efforts, the GCC should adopt a threefold posture: reject the concept of the "security vacuum" in the gulf; take a neutral position toward disputes involving neighboring states; and cooperate with all regimes in the Persian Gulf and Arabian Peninsula regions.

The future of the GCC would be influenced, according to Dr. Mubarak, by several factors, including:

Recent regressive developments in the Iranian revolution.
The Iraq-Iran war.
The continuing dependence of the industrial world on gulf oil.
Soviet-U.S. rivalry and the Soviet invasion of Afghanistan.
The establishment of Soviet and U.S. military base and facilities
     in the region.
The Arab-Israeli conflict.
The Arab cold war and the continuing disputes among different Arab
     regimes.

The argument that the GCC will continue to be influenced by
factors outside the control of the member states was also repeated
by another member of the gulf elites. 'Abdul Muhsin Taqi Muzaffar,
secretary-general of the Arab Planning Institute in Kuwait, cautioned
the GCC to be aware of and avoid potentially destructive factors.
Four such factors could exist: (1) gulf cooperation could be reduced
just to the security area without any social or economic content;
(2) border disputes could hinder gulf cooperation; (3) this cooperative scheme could represent only the rulers rather than their peoples;
and (4) the absence of Iraq and the Yemens could diminish the significance of the GCC as a truly regional organization.[17] Although the
foundations for cooperation are present, it is possible for the GCC
to fail if it is not supported by the peoples of the region.

On the other hand, Dr. Muhammad 'Abdul Ghani Sa'udi, professor of political geography at the University of Kuwait, took a
more pragmatic approach to regional cooperation.[18] He said that
the gulf's strategic, social, economic, and political features have
helped to produce regional cooperation. In view of the outside
world's interest in and dependence on gulf oil, cooperation among
local states is the only logical course of action. In order to preserve themselves in view of their small size, small indigenous population, and oil-generated wealth, gulf states find themselves pushed
into cooperation. Dr. Sa'udi also stated that cooperation would help
the gulf maintain good relations with the United States, once U.S.
policy makers agree on the components of U.S. policy in the gulf.

The last to be interviewed in this series of articles was Nazih
Barqawi, a Kuwaiti economist.[19] His main point is that gulf cooperation will have both positive and negative ramifications. The
current abundant wealth of liquid assets will have a positive impact
on regional cooperation in the short run, but the picture is not that
clear once the oil resources are depleted. On the negative side,
gulf states, though rich in oil revenues, are poor in productive and
economic infrastructures.

A thoughtful analysis of the Gulf Cooperation Council was presented in a two-part article in al-Khaleej newspaper on September 1,

1981 by Dr. Omar Ibrahim al-Khatib.[20] He envisioned the GCC as operating in three concentric circles: the local (internal) circle, the regional circle, and the Arab/international circle.

In the local circle, the GCC document discussed the establishment of similar systems among the member states in the fields of economics, finance, commerce, education, culture, social welfare, and health, but it ignored the political aspect. Two central issues are involved here: the need to emphasize the importance of written permanent constitutions as the foundation of modern nation-states; and the need to emphasize the importance of popular participation in government on a democratic basis, through free and open elections.

On the regional level, four issues should be addressed, according to Dr. al-Khatib.

1. Membership in the GCC. The document seems to have prevented the entry of any new members. Other countries such as Iraq, North Yemen, and South Yemen should have the opportunity to join if they so desire. Preventing new membership was perhaps what encouraged South Yemen to enter into some sort of alliance with Libya and Ethiopia, two nongulf states.

2. Security in the gulf and the Indian Ocean. Despite the official rhetoric regarding keeping the gulf outside of superpower struggle, some GCC members still offer military "facilities" to outside powers. Furthermore, in spite of official statements supporting neutrality, some GCC members still endorse a foreign policy that favors a specific superpower at the expense of others. Finally, although the GCC has spoken out against foreign military presence in the region, and although some GCC members have strongly condemned the Soviet military presence in Afghanistan, no similar statements have been made regarding U.S. military presence in some countries bordering on the Persian Gulf, Red Sea, and Indian Ocean.

3. The Iran-Iraq war. The GCC seems to be totally ineffective in settling the Iraq-Iran war. At least for geopolitical reasons, the GCC should expend every effort to settle this war, which might engulf neighboring states as well.

4. Oil. Dr. al-Khatib maintains that the GCC's stand on a unified oil policy has been ineffective. In fact, very little coordination, if any, has occurred in the area of oil production, pricing, and marketing.

In the Arab/international circle, Dr. al-Khatib suggested that the GCC state: (a) the establishment of the GCC is in accordance with the Arab League's goals and aspirations; (b) the GCC supports the Palestinians and recognizes the PLO as the sole representative of the Palestinian people; and (c) the tragic events in Lebanon are "part and parcel of a comprehensive American conspiracy against the Arab world for the purpose of liquidating the Palestinian resistance and eliminating the chances of PLO to play any meaningful political role."[21] Dr. al-Khatib also called on the GCC to encourage Western Europe to take a position more independent of the U.S. stand on the Palestinian conflict.

In view of the preceding statements on the GCC, it is possible to make the following comments. First, although the Gulf Cooperation Council is a positive step toward regional collective action, it is too early to judge the efficacy of this council or to predict its long-term success. Second, government officials in the six member states tend to be strong supporters of the GCC, while the elites are more cautious in their support. Third, in their analysis of the GCC, gulf intellectuals seem to agree that the GCC should: promote Arab unity, encourage popular participation in government, bridge the gap between the rulers and their peoples, support the Palestinian people, encourage a more equitable distribution of wealth, chart a more neutral course for the gulf in international relations, and discourage any close military relations with the superpowers that would invite any foreign military presence in the region.

THE GULF COOPERATION COUNCIL
AND REGIONAL SECURITY

Since its formation in May 1981, the GCC has been equated with the preservation of the Persian Gulf's security and stability. Although committees have been established to coordinate social, economic, cultural, and informational activities among the member states, most of the activities of the GCC have focused on security matters.

Any analysis of the GCC's position on gulf security raises the following questions:

What does security mean? Whose security is involved? Whose interests does it serve?

If regional security is threatened, who should define the nature of such a threat? What action should be taken to neutralize such a threat and by whom?

Can gulf security be realistically separated from internal stability? If it cannot, is internal stability synonymous with the continued survival of the regimes presently in power? If it is, what measures, both immediate and long-term, should be adopted by these regimes to preserve themselves?

Gulf officials have indicated that local states must be directly involved in any search for answers to these questions, and that it would be futile for any outside power, no matter how friendly, to answer these questions without meaningful consultation with the local states.

Reflecting on the concepts of regional security and stability since the establishment of the Gulf Cooperation Council, it is possible to identify three different definitions of security. Two of these reflect internal views, while the third is mostly Western in orientation. The Western concept of gulf security is basically status quo oriented, meaning a continuation of family regimes with strong military and economic ties to the United States and to other Western countries. Under such an arrangement, the United States promises to provide security if the gulf faces a serious Soviet threat, either directly or by proxy. For Western security to function effectively in such a scenario, U.S. armed forces should have the capability of being deployed in the region expeditiously. These forces would either be positioned in the region (on land or over the horizon) or would be airlifted from U.S. bases.

A secure and/or stable gulf from Washington's point of view would mean: a continued survival of the present regimes; free flow of oil through the Strait of Hormuz; containment of the Iranian Islamic revolution; containment of Soviet activities in the region; and a conscious separation of the Palestinian conflict from gulf security issues.

The definition of regional security by the Persian Gulf countries, on the other hand, seems to be different from that advanced by the United States and some of its European allies. Most gulf officials perceive regional security as keeping the region aloof from superpower rivalry and foreign military bases. They feel that they must be the primary guarantors of regional security, which they would provide through cooperative efforts. Hence, the Gulf Cooperation Council is seen as the most effective vehicle for the protection of gulf security and regional stability. The immediate overwhelming support that gulf leaders offered Bahrain in mid-December 1981 upon the discovery of an antiregime plot in that country strongly illustrates this point. [22] The perception of gulf leaders regarding regional security seems to differ from that of the United States only in focus and orientation. Whereas the U.S. concept reflects a global balance of power between the two superpowers, regional security to gulf leaders means a preservation of the family-controlled status quo.

In order to illustrate the gulf countries' official view of regional security, it might be useful to examine the following statements. Reacting to the report from Bahrain that the plot was devised in Iran, Crown Prince Fahd of Saudi Arabia stated that "the Arab states of the Gulf will defend themselves against any threat to

Gulf security."[23] In a similar vein, Shaikh Muhammad bin Mubarak al-Khalifa, the foreign minister of Bahrain, indicated that "the people of the Gulf are best suited to defend the region without any need for foreign military bases."[24] A similar position was expressed by the Kuwaiti defense minister, Shaikh Salim al-Sabah in August 1981. He indicated that the gulf countries "are capable of protecting their security by themselves."[25]

The task of protecting gulf security has apparently been assigned to the Gulf Cooperation Council. Most of the official statements since November 1981 have stressed the role of the GCC in regional security. In an interview in al-Siyasa newspaper of Kuwait, the Saudi Arabian defense minister, Prince Sultan ibn 'Abd al-'Aziz, said that the GCC had agreed to set up an "advanced defense group to coordinate the defenses of the GCC countries."[26]

At the conclusion of the GCC summit on November 11, 1981, an official statement indicated that the six heads of state agreed on the following points:

The serenity and stability of the gulf are the responsibility of its states.

Any attempt by the superpowers to interfere in the gulf region should be opposed if it would result in a conflict that is not in agreement with the interests of the gulf states and its people.

The region should avoid entanglement in international conflicts; this refers especially to the presence of military fleets and foreign bases.[27]

In praising the same GCC summit, the amir of Qatar, Shaikh Khalifa bin Hamad al-Thani, said that the summit was a milestone for the coordination of gulf resources toward the security, stability, progress, and prosperity of the region.[28] At that summit, the GCC agreed to create a common air defense system.[29] This fact was confirmed more recently by Shaikh Hamad bin Isa al-Khalifa, Bahrain's heir apparent and minister of defense. He indicated also that he was optimistic about military coordination among the GCC states. He stated that the gulf's security was the responsibility of its citizens, that the GCC has reached an understanding on coordinating the air defense of the region, and that aerial coverage does indeed exist in case of emergency.[30]

Following the coup attempt, Bahrain's interior minister, Shaikh Muhammad bin Khalifa al-Khalifa, called on the GCC to form a rapid deployment force to protect the region's wealth and safeguard its peace and security. He indicated that "funds are available to form such a force."[31] The interior minister also announced that there is complete coordination on security matters with other GCC countries.[32] The Qatari interior minister, Shaikh Khalid bin Hamad al-Thani, supported the idea of a rapid deployment force for GCC countries and urged the signing of a collective security agreement.[33]

In his address to the opening session of the Federal National Council on December 28, 1981, the president of the United Arab Emirates, Shaikh Zayed al-Nhayyan, linked the GCC to gulf security. He said that, "We view the establishment of the GCC as vital for the member countries. . . . It is an important beginning in reinforcing cooperation among the Gulf countries so that they can defend themselves, unify their ranks, ensure their common interests and achieve their national aspirations in order to strengthen the bases of stability and progress for all area peoples."[34]

The third perception of regional security is that of gulf elites (intellectuals, journalists, reform-oriented businessmen, students, and labor leaders). Briefly, this perception equates security with the survival of the regimes themselves, meaning that unless the people are brought into the governing process, regional security will always be problematic.

In contrast to these official perceptions of security, many intellectuals have equated security with improving the lot of the average citizen. A representative sample of this genre is an article that appeared in al-Qabas in May 1981. Among the points made in the article were:

1. Security, as envisioned by gulf regimes, serves to preserve those regimes in power.

2. It is impossible to achieve security without social, political, and economic stability for the peoples of the area. This means that mutual respect should exist between the governments and the peoples.

3. True security can be achieved through rejecting foreign military presence in the gulf, sharing political power with the people according to an equitable and orderly system of political participation, distributing wealth on the basis of social justice, national economic planning, and finally through a majority rule that respects the rights of the minority.[35] These views were shared by several other intellectuals at a special symposium held in Sharja (United Arab Emirates) in April 1981.[36]

REFLECTIONS ON GULF COOPERATION
AND SECURITY

The region's political, intellectual, and business leaders are determined to play a serious role in regional stability and security.

Nor is there much doubt that a regional perception of the concepts of security and stability exists and that it differs from the one generally held by outside powers. The Gulf Cooperation Council is an attempt by six family-ruled states to take a collective, and hence more influential, position on questions of regional security, stability, and economic integration. Indeed, the survival of the individual regimes, as demonstrated in Bahrain, dictates that collective action be taken. Regional cooperation is therefore presented as an appropriate response to meet these needs.

Despite the rhetoric of self-reliance and "gulfanization" of regional security, all of the GCC states continue to maintain fairly strong economic and military relations with the United States and Western Europe. Rejection of military bases has not deterred gulf leaders from purchasing huge volumes of arms from the United States and its allies, nor from relying on hundreds of United States' and European military consultants to build local military infra- structures.

Yet it would be erroneous on the part of U.S. policy makers to interpret the gulf states' westward leaning as an indication of a consensus on the basic concepts of security and stability. Friend- ship with the West does not negate the determination of these coun- tries to cooperate with each other and to approach their problems from Arab and Islamic perspectives. For example, an Arab per- spective takes Palestine into consideration, and an Islamic perspec- tive cannot ignore Jerusalem. Both are under an Israeli occupation that appears to be supported, at least politically if not juridically, by the United States.

What should be of more concern to U.S. defenders of the status quo policy is the increasing involvement of gulf elites in the debate on regional security and stability. This involvement is not restricted to university professors. As we have seen above, many middle-class businessmen, journalists, and other professionals share similar definitions of regional cooperation, security, and stability.

The elite groups connect regional security and internal stabil- ity. They maintain that internal stability can endure only through political participation, social justice, and an equitable distribution of wealth. Another connection is between gulf security and the Palestinian conflict; this is something that official statements, at least publicly, have confirmed.

There is also an emerging consensus among the intellectuals that the Gulf Cooperation Council and similar cooperative arrange- ments are primarily designed to preserve the present regimes in power. The prompt reaction of other states to the antiregime plot in Bahrain was cited by some elites as an illustration of the nervousness of these governments. This confirmed their suspicions that the GCC is basically a collective security arrangement and is only secondarily interested in the betterment of the peoples of the area.

On the optimistic side, a new tendency toward cooperation is emerging in the gulf states among leaders and peoples alike. Evidence is available to indicate that this cooperation is being conducted on many levels and in many fields. Economic cooperation is already several years old, and some political cooperation has also occurred. An example of other forms of cooperation is the support given to the eight-point Arab National Charter proposed by Iraq on February 8, 1980. The charter, whose points are listed below, enjoins Arab states from waging war against each other and encourages them to settle their disputes peacefully. The charter, which has been endorsed by all gulf Arab states, seems to embody principles similar to those undergirding the GCC. It is quoted here for purposes of comparison with the provisions of the GCC already discussed.

THE ARAB NATIONAL CHARTER
February 8, 1980

1. The presence in the Arab homeland of any foreign troops or military forces shall be rejected and no facilities for the use of Arab territory shall be extended to them in any form or under any pretext or cover. Any Arab regime that fails to comply with this principle shall be proscribed and boycotted both economically and politically, as well as politically opposed by all available means.

2. The recourse to armed force by one Arab state against another Arab state shall be prohibited, and any dispute arising between Arab states shall be resolved by peaceful means in accordance with the principles of joint Arab action and the higher Arab interest.

3. The principle embodied in Article 2 shall apply to the relations of the Arab nation and its constituent states with neighboring countries, with recourse to armed force in any disputes arising with these countries prohibited except in the case of self-defense or the defense of sovereignty against threats that affect the security and vital interests of the Arab states.

4. All the Arab states shall collaborate in opposing any aggression or violation by any foreign power directed against the territorial sovereignty of any Arab

state or the waging of war against any Arab state. All
the Arab states shall act together in facing up to and
repelling such aggression or violation by every available means including military action, collective political and economic boycotts, or action in other fields as
the need arises and in accordance with the dictates of
the national interest.

5. The Arab states reaffirm their adherence to
international law and practice in so far as concerns the
use of air space, waterways and land routes by any
state not in a state of war with any Arab state.

6. The Arab states shall steer clear of the
arena of international conflicts and wars, and shall
maintain strict neutrality and non-alignment vis-a-vis
any party to a conflict or war, provided that none of
the parties to such conflicts and wars shall violate
Arab territorial sovereignty or the established rights
of the Arab states as guaranteed by international law
and practice. The Arab states shall prohibit any involvement by their armed forces, partially or totally,
in wars or armed disputes in the area or outside it on
behalf of any state or foreign party.

7. The Arab states undertake to establish close
economic ties between each other in such a manner as
to make possible the creation of a common foundation
for an advanced and unified Arab economic structure.

8. In putting forward the principles of this charter, Iraq reaffirms its readiness to assume the commitments implicit in it towards all Arab states or any
party that adheres to it, and is prepared to discuss it
with the other Arab states and would welcome any suggestions that would reinforce its effectiveness. [37]

This charter seems to have been ignored by Iraq in its war
with Iran, but most of its provisions, particularly the first one regarding foreign military presence in Arab lands, continue to be supported by gulf Arab states. Before the war, some gulf leaders had
viewed the charter as a vehicle through which Iraq would both extricate itself from the Soviet orbit and at the same time chart a moderate course toward its Arab neighbors in the south. However, Iraq's
preoccupation with the war has forestalled any southward movement.

NOTES

1. Arab Shipbuilding and Repair Yard Co., Annual Review 1980 (Bahrain), 1981.
2. Richard D. Erb and Nabil al-Shawaf, "Building on Existing Linkages in the Middle East" (Washington, D.C.: American Enterprise Institute, 1978), p. 20. Unpublished.
3. Ibid., pp. 41-44.
4. Akhbar al-Khaleej (Bahrain), May 27, 1981, p. 3.
5. Ibid., May 28, 1981, p. 7.
6. al-Adwa' (Bahrain), May 30, 1981, p. 3.
7. Ibid., p. 7.
8. Washington Post, February 27, 1981, p. A25.
9. Monday Morning (Beirut), July 20-26, 1981, pp. 20-26; translated in FBIS 5 (August 6, 1981):C1-5.
10. Akhbar al-Khaleej (Bahrain), June 23, 1981, p. 3.
11. al-Qabas (Kuwait), February 2-28, 1981.
12. Ibid., February 7, 1981, p. 5.
13. Ibid., February 8, 1981, p. 5.
14. Ibid., February 10, 1981, p. 5.
15. Ibid., February 11, 1981, p. 10.
16. Ibid., February 12, 1981, p. 10.
17. Ibid., February 13, 1981, p. 10.
18. Ibid., February 17, 1981, p. 10.
19. Ibid., February 28, 1981, p. 5.
20. al-Khaleej (Dubai), September 1, 1981, p. 3.
21. Ibid., September 2, 1981, p. 3.
22. "Terror Plot Arms Found," Gulf Mirror (Bahrain), December 19-23, 1981, p. 1.
23. Akhbar al-Khaleej (Bahrain), December 27, 1981, p. 1.
24. al-Adwa' (Bahrain), January 17, 1981, p. 3.
25. FBIS 5 (August 6, 1981):C9.
26. Ibid. 5 (November 5, 1981):C5.
27. Ibid. 5 (November 12, 1981):C4.
28. Ibid. 5 (November 13, 1981):C2.
29. Ibid. 5 (November 13, 1981):C1.
30. al-Adwa' (Bahrain), February 6, 1982, p. 1; FBIS 5 (February 12, 1982):C1-3.
31. FBIS 5 (December 23, 1981):C1.
32. Ibid. 5 (December 28, 1981):C1.
33. Ibid. 5 (December 28, 1981):C3.
34. Ibid. 5 (December 30, 1981):C11.
35. al-Qabas (Kuwait), May 24, 1981, pp. 1, 27.
36. al-Khaleej (Dubai), April 20, 1981, pp. 3, 5.
37. The Middle East (London), April 1980, p. 20.

4

THE PALESTINIAN CONFLICT
AND THE GULF

INTRODUCTION: PRINCIPLES OF SAUDI POLICY

The October 1973 War forged the first major links between
the Palestinian conflict and Persian Gulf politics, and it highlighted
the triangular relationship between the United States, Israel (including the Palestinian conflict), and the gulf. Public and private
statements from the Palestinian leadership, gulf rulers, and U.S.
government foreign policy officials since the mid-1970s have underscored this triangle. The state most conspicuously involved in this
relationship has been Saudi Arabia. Other Arab gulf states have
mostly fallen in behind the Saudis; hence, the analysis in this section is primarily concerned with Saudi policies. It can be argued
that even before the October War Saudi foreign policy included a
strong stand on the Palestinian conflict, but the intensity of its
position has varied with the period, the crisis, and the location of
the crisis. However, Saudi diplomacy on Palestine has consistently
considered six cardinal principles:

1. Muslims should be able to worship in Jerusalem freely,
and East Jerusalem must be preserved as an Arab city, culturally
and politically.
2. The mainstream ideological character of the Palestinian
movement must be moderate, be under a moderate leadership, and
avoid foreign radical ideologies (presumably Soviet).
3. The Palestinian movement must not be under the control
of any one Arab country to the exclusion of others, and the movement should not be allowed to chart a course independent of the
mainstream Arab position, regardless of how that position may be
defined at the moment.

4. A primary objective of Saudi diplomacy is to minimize Palestinian relations with and dependency on the Soviet Union and to emphasize the potential role of the United States in effecting a settlement.

5. Saudi Arabia's endorsement of Palestinian political/ nationalistic objectives should not adversely affect its special relationship with the United States. By the same token, Palestinian armed resistance, military operations, or ideological disputes should not impair gulf stability.

6. Negotiation is the only viable resolution of the Palestine conflict. These negotiations should involve: (a) United Nations Resolutions 242 and 338; (b) Israeli withdrawal from territories occupied since 1967; (c) affirmation of the principle of self-determination for the Palestinian people; and (d) a respect for all states including Israel.

Saudi Arabia's diplomacy concerning Palestine has been more or less supported by other gulf states and recently through the Gulf Cooperation Council. This diplomacy has been pursued, albeit unobtrusively, by three avenues: the Arab states, the Muslim world, and the United States. Through the Arab states, Saudi Arabia has attempted to accomplish two objectives: first, to maintain the conflict within the Arab state system, which implies that the Palestinian people can regain their national rights through diplomacy practiced by Arab states; and second, to contain the conflict within the moderate Arab mainstream, which again implies that radicalism and rejectionism could not resolve the conflict. Radical ideologies and rejectionist states have been incapable of forcing Israel to withdraw from Arab lands or to restore national rights to the Palestinians.

On the Islamic front, Saudi diplomacy concerning Palestine has been more forceful. In the numerous meetings of Muslim heads of state, Saudi leaders have sought to "Islamicize" the conflict by drawing attention to Jerusalem as a symbol of the world of Islam and as a city under occupation. The late King Faisal had often expressed his wish "to pray in Jerusalem." Actions by successive Israeli governments such as the annexation of the eastern sector of Jerusalem, excavations in the Old City, and the demolition of old homes near the Mosque of Omar and the Dome of the Rock Mosque have been frequently cited by Saudi spokesmen to underscore their concerns for the Muslim nature of the city, and by inference of the entire conflict. The refusal of the Israeli government to allow the Arab residents of East Jerusalem to vote in any West Bank national election under the Camp David Accords has also been cited by Saudi Arabia as illustrating Israel's policy to change the physical and demographic nature of Jerusalem.

Saudi Arabia has endeavored to persuade U.S. policy makers that: (1) Saudi friendship toward the United States is both genuine and beneficial (economically and strategically); (2) Washington's gulf interests would be better served through this friendship; and (3) such a friendship would be immeasurably strengthened by a United States-initiated resolution of the Palestinian conflict. Saudi Arabia's realistic assessment of the United States reflects a Saudi belief that, because of the special relationship between Washington and Tel Aviv, the United States is the only nation capable of initiating a settlement.

Underlying this assessment is the Saudi view that because of the disparity in the current balance of power in Israel's favor and because of Israel's refusal to address the heart of the Palestinian problem, a genuine process of negotiation cannot begin with the parties themselves. An outside influence must be utilized; such an influence can only come from the United States. It is interesting to note that the Saudi view of the U.S. role in the peace process is similar to that held by President Anwar Sadat of Egypt between 1973 and 1978.

By pursuing their policy on Palestine through the three avenues stated above, Saudi foreign policy makers seem to have a global perspective of the conflict. By forging the three sides (the Arab, the Islamic, and the United States) into one logical whole Saudi Arabia seems to be attempting to build an "arc of strategic consensus" of its own. According to this scenario, the level of Arab-U.S. relations would be intensified to the level of Israeli-U.S. relations, thereby enticing Washington to view its interests in the Arab world, particularly in the gulf, with the same sense of urgency that it perceives its Israeli interests. If this occurs, the Saudis hope that Washington's gulf Arab partners would begin to occupy a position in U.S. long-range policy planning similar to the one that Israel already occupies. Again, this approach parallels that taken by Sadat.

Saudi policy on Palestine since the June 1967 war has gone through several stages, but Saudi officials have always maintained that these stages have only reflected changing circumstances and tactics. The constancy of these principles has not changed. Four major stages of policy development can be identified.

SAUDI PERCEPTIONS AND POLICIES, 1967-73

In the period following the 1967 war, with the humiliating Arab defeat, the Israeli occupation of the Golan Heights, the Sinai, and the West Bank and Gaza, Saudi Arabia and the rest of the Arab world reacted to the defeat with the "three no's" statement. In the communiqué of the Arab summit conference on September 1, 1967, held at Khartoum, Sudan, the Arab heads of state agreed:

> to unite their political efforts on the international and diplomatic level to eliminate the effects of the aggression and to ensure the withdrawal of the aggressive Israeli forces from the Arab lands which have been occupied since the 5 June aggression. This will be done within the framework of the main principles to which the Arab states adhere, namely: no peace with Israel, no recognition of Israel, no negotiations with it, and adherence to the rights of the Palestinian people in their country.[1]

In the aftermath of the Khartoum summit, Saudi Arabia's foreign policy concerning the Palestinian conflict incorporated three major goals: to provide financial support for Egypt, Syria, and Jordan for economic development and defense; to generate concern in the Islamic world over Israeli occupation of Jerusalem; and to resist pressures from Arab nationalists to adopt a radical posture in its dealings with the West, particularly with the United States. Internationally, Saudi Arabia has consistently supported Security Council Resolution 242 of November 22, 1967. Among other things, the resolution emphasized "the inadmissibility of the acquisition of territory by war," affirmed the need to establish "a just and lasting peace in the Middle East . . ." which would include "the withdrawal of Israel from territories occupied during the war and respect for the sovereignty, territorial integrity and political independence of every State in the area. . . ."[2]

During this period, Saudi Arabia's King Faisal took a strong position against Israeli policies in East Jerusalem, even appealing to the Muslim world to declare a jihad (holy war) for the liberation of the sacred places.[3] At the same time, Saudi Arabia's financial support was extended to Nasser of Egypt in his "war of attrition" with Israel, to Yasser Arafat in his rise to prominence within the Palestine Liberation Organization (PLO), and even to King Hussein of Jordan in his attempt to curb the rising power of the PLO within Jordan. Saudi Arabia, like most other Arab states, did not necessarily condemn King Hussein's bloody confrontation with the Palestinians in "Black September" 1970.

On the Persian Gulf side, the Palestinian conflict played a negligible role in regional politics during the 1967–73 period, until the October War. Saudi Arabia's regional foreign policy supported the establishment of a federated state among gulf amirates and the independence of other states. At the same time, Saudi Arabia opposed the rise of leftist movements in the gulf, particularly the Popular Front for the Liberation of Oman and the Arabian Gulf on the grounds that these leftist ideologies were mostly communist inspired and supported. In this regard, Saudi Arabia did not object to, but even tacitly supported, the emphasis on regional security and stability in the gulf by the United States that emerged in the 1972 official statements from Washington. [4] Nor did the Saudis object to the evolving United States-Iranian connection under the umbrella of the Nixon Doctrine aiming at the creation of a special brand of Pax Persiana under the leadership of the Shah. Indeed, by the mid-1970s, Iranian troops were deployed in Oman to help the Sultan fight the leftist Dhufari rebels in that country.

The anticommunist component of Saudi foreign policy also extended to Saudi relations with Egypt in that King Faisal played an influential role in encouraging President Sadat in the 1971-72 period to reduce his dependence on the Soviet Union and ultimately to break away from the Soviets. Sadat's dismissal of Soviet advisers in 1972 was to a large extent encouraged and supported by Saudi Arabia. In a sense, that was the first major effort on the part of Saudi Arabia to start an Egyptian-United States dialogue, thereby initiating a triangular relationship involving the United States, the Arab-Israeli conflict through Egypt, and the gulf through Saudi Arabia. This process, of course, accelerated rapidly with the eruption of the October War and the ensuing oil embargo.

SAUDI PERCEPTIONS AND POLICIES, 1973-SUMMER 1977

The linkage between the Palestinian conflict and the Persian Gulf reached new heights in the aftermath of the October 1973 War. Although the record has not been fully revealed, it is believed that Saudi Arabia, with the personal involvement of King Faisal, supported President Sadat's war policy in 1973. The Saudis, like the Egyptian leadership, viewed the war as a tool of diplomacy that would accomplish several goals: (1) it would create a positive psychological disposition among the Arabs by erasing the humiliation of the 1967 defeat; (2) it would redress the balance of power between Israel and the Arabs; (3) it would create a more conducive atmosphere for negotiations between Egypt and Israel, particularly if Egypt's war effort could puncture Israel's military invincibility; (4) it would involve the superpowers more directly in the conflict, both diplomatically and militarily; and (5) as a corollary to the previous point, the war would somehow force the United States to enter the negotiation process as a "full partner."

It was an ambitious plan, but although the war turned against Egypt after the third day of the fighting, Sadat did accomplish most, if not all, of his objectives. The U.S. military airlift to Israel, for the purpose of resupplying Israeli losses on the battlefield unwittingly abetted Sadat's objectives. The United States' direct involvement meant that Washington would exert a new kind of influence on Israel, that Washington would enter the negotiations directly to save the Egyptian Third Army and move toward a more comprehensive peace, and that by resupplying Israel through the airlift, Washington would force the Arab world, particularly Saudi Arabia, to react much more forcefully than before. Negotiations did start, and the United States entered the process as more than a mediator. Through the oil embargo and the massive aid to Egypt and Syria, Saudi Arabia demonstrated forcefully that the politics of oil and the politics of Palestine were now inextricably linked.

The October War therefore remolded Middle East politics into a triangular shape held together by interconnected linkages: the centrality of the Palestinian issue to the Arab-Israeli dispute; the involvement of the gulf in the Palestinian conflict; and the United States' essential role in the reestablishment of regional order based on the new realities.

The statement issued at the conclusion of the OAPEC meeting on October 17, 1973 vividly illustrates these links. The statement indicated that the 5 percent monthly reduction in oil production that was adopted at that meeting was designed "to compel Israel to withdraw from our occupied lands and make the United States aware of the exorbitant price the great industrial states are paying as a result of its blind and unlimited support for Israel."[5]

The Saudi decision in October 1973 to relate the flow of oil to U.S. policy on the Palestinian conflict marked a pronounced deviation from previous practices. This decision underscored three basic assumptions that continue to undergird the United States-Persian Gulf-Palestinian connections: that "Arab oil production can no longer be treated separately from Arab national issues, more particularly the Palestine problem"; that "smoothly functioning economic relations will follow only if outstanding political conflicts are resolved"; and that "the United States, as a major industrial country and as a superpower directly concerned with international peace and security" must examine other options in dealing with the Arab-Israeli conflict.[6] As will be shown below, the United States responded to these developments with new policies. The oil embargo was finally lifted on March 18, 1974.

These new policies, which included strong efforts by the United States and especially by the Secretary of State Henry Kissinger, produced three disengagement agreements: two were in the Sinai between Israel and Egypt (January 15, 1974 and September 1, 1975), and one was on the Golan Heights between Israel and Syria on May 31, 1974. Saudi Arabia and the other gulf states supported the three disengagement agreements and even played a somewhat active role in facilitating Kissinger's negotiations.

Beyond the specific demarcation lines negotiated in the agreements, the most interesting point was the commitment of the signatories to comprehensive peace between Israel and the Arab estates. Consider the following references in the agreements to a comprehensive peace:

Article D of the First Sinai Disengagement Agreement states:

This agreement is not regarded by Egypt and Israel as a final peace agreement. It constitutes a first step toward a final, just and durable peace according to the provisions of Security Council Resolution 338 and within the framework of the Geneva Conference.[7]

Article H of the Golan Heights Disengagement Agreement states:

This agreement is not a peace agreement. It is a step toward a just and durable peace on the basis of Security Council Resolution 338 dated October 22, 1973.[8]

Article VIII of the Second Sinai Disengagement Agreement makes similar points:

(1) This agreement is regarded by the parties as a significant step toward a just and lasting peace. It is not a final peace agreement.
(2) The parties shall continue their efforts to negotiate a final peace agreement within the framework of the Geneva peace conference in accordance with Security Council Resolution 338.[9]

Saudi Arabia endorsed these agreements as well as Security Council Resolution 338 itself. In addition to calling on the conflicting parties to implement Security Council Resolution 242 (1967), Resolution 338 (Section 3) stated that:

immediately and concurrently with the cease-fire, negotiations shall start between the parties concerned under appropriate auspices aimed at establishing a just and durable peace in the Middle East.[10]

Saudi diplomacy in the mid-1970s evolved in several directions that were related to each other in an intricate balance of Palestinian moderation and U.S. involvement. Between June 1974 and September 1977, Saudi diplomacy pursued three major courses of action simultaneously:

1. Establishing a special economic, financial, and security relationship with the United States, starting with the United States-Saudi Arabia Joint Commission founded on June 8, 1974 and signed by Secretary Kissinger and Crown Prince Fahd. Four working groups were established under the joint commission system for economic cooperation: industrialization, manpower and education, science and technology, and agriculture.[11] In the security area, sales of U.S. arms to Saudi Arabia and other gulf Arab states in 1974-75 reached new levels, totaling hundreds of millions of dollars.[12]

2. Encouraging the United States to play a central role in resolving the Palestinian conflict by considering the national rights of the Palestinian people, as well as the security demands of Israel, and by requiring Israeli withdrawal from the occupied territories as dictated by Security Council Resolution 242. The Saudi position revolved around three arguments: the issue of Palestine is central to questions of war and peace in the region; U.S. interests ultimately will be adversely affected by continued conflict; if the U.S. position would tilt toward a solution aiming at a "just and durable peace," a moderating Arab (and Palestinian) position would emerge. Briefly, the Saudis argued that a just peace would mean a recognition of Palestinian national rights (not necessarily a state) and that the more Washington became involved in a comprehensive peace process, the more Arab moderation would be forthcoming; involvement and moderation were presented as two sides of the same coin.

3. The final course of action pursued by Saudi diplomacy during the 1974-77 period was to support the rising stature of the Palestine Liberation Organization as the legitimate representative of the Palestinian people. Thus for the first time the Palestinians would be recognized as a party to the conflict. The Saudis maintained that the Arab-Israeli conflict was not just between Israel and the Arab states on a state-to-state basis but was a conflict between Israel and the Palestinians. Any future peace negotiations must involve Palestinian representatives. The centrality of the Palestinian conflict to regional stability now involved an acceptance of the centrality of the Palestinian leadership in peace negotiations.

In its diplomatic maneuvering, Saudi diplomacy had to merge two responsibilities: to help a moderate Palestinian leadership emerge and maintain control of the PLO, and secondly to prevent the leadership from falling under the influence of any one Arab state. In response to the first responsibility, Saudi Arabia increased its financial support for the PLO under Yasser Arafat and Fateh and its diplomatic tempo within the Arab and Islamic camps on behalf of the PLO. Financial aid strengthened the moderate elements within the PLO in their quest for a diplomatic solution to the conflict, as opposed to the hitherto unquestioned strategy of an "armed struggle." The moderate position was also enhanced vis-à-vis the radical groups within the organization. On the diplomatic front, the Saudi effort brought recognition to the PLO on the regional and international levels.

Saudi three-pronged diplomacy in this period, which was based on Palestinian moderation, Palestinian recognition, and U.S. involvement, was for the most part successful. As examples of this success consider the following.

Concerning Palestinian moderation, the first tangible signal was the ten-point political program adopted by the Palestine National Council on June 9, 1974. Although a cursory reading of this program might not indicate any changes in the PLO's position, a closer look at specific words used would give a different interpretation. Some "code" phrases in the second point of the program indicated two major changes in the PLO's strategy: (1) that "armed struggle" is not the only available means of regaining Palestinian national rights; and (2) that the PLO would be willing to establish a "national authority" on any part of Palestine that is liberated from Israeli occupation. Translated from the Middle Eastern political lexicon, these statements mean that the PLO was seeking a diplomatic solution through the creation of a Palestinian state in the occupied territories as soon as occupation is terminated. This interpretation of Article 2 of the program prompted talk of a Palestinian state on the West Bank and Gaza. Article 2 states:

> The Liberation Organization will employ all means, and first and foremost armed struggle, to liberate Palestinian territory and to establish the independent combatant national authority for the people over every part of Palestinian territory that is liberated. This will require further changes being effected in the balance of power in favor of our people and their struggle.[13] (Emphasis added.)

Concerning Palestinian recognition, the PLO was able in 1974-75 to obtain recognition from major regional and international bodies through Saudi, Persian Gulf, and Arab diplomacy. Of course, the most significant recognition was obtained at the seventh Arab League summit in Rabat, Morocco on October 29, 1974. The summit affirmed, among other things:

> the right of the Palestinian people to establish an independent national authority under the command of the Palestine Liberation Organization, the sole legitimate representative of the Palestinian people, in any Palestinian territory that is liberated. This authority, once it is established, shall enjoy the support of the Arab states in all fields and at all levels.[14] (Emphasis added).

Through this resolution, the Arab heads of state bestowed upon the PLO the status of a government in exile with the rights and privileges of a state. During October and November of that same year, the PLO registered several successes at the United Nations. On October 14, 1974, the U.N. General Assembly invited "the Palestine Liberation Organization, the representative of the Palestinian people, to participate in the deliberations of the General Assembly on the question of Palestine in plenary meetings."[15] On November 22, 1974, the U.N. General Assembly requested the secretary-general "to establish contacts with the Palestine Liberation Organization on all matters concerning the question of Palestine."[16] In another resolution on the same day, the General Assembly resolved to invite the PLO "to participate in the sessions and the work of the General Assembly . . . [and] in the sessions and work of all international conferences convened under the auspices of the General Assembly in the capacity of observer."[17]

On the centrality of the Palestinian conflict to United States foreign policy makers, numerous statements were made by Washington in the 1970s by presidents and State Department officials linking the Palestinian conflict to U.S. national interest in the gulf. Among the first, and most quoted, statement is the testimony of the former deputy assistant secretary of state for Near Eastern and South Asian affairs, Harold Saunders, in the U.S. Congress on November 12, 1975. Saunders stated in part that:

> We have also repeatedly stated that the legitimate interests of the Palestinian Arabs must be taken into account in the negotiation of an Arab-Israeli peace. In many ways, the Palestinian dimension of the Arab-Israeli conflict is the heart of that conflict. Final resolutions of the problems arising from the partition of Palestine, the establishment of the State of Israel, and Arab

opposition to those events will not be possible until
agreement is reached defining a just and permanent
status for the Arab peoples who consider themselves
Palestinians.[18]

Less than two years later, President Carter, in a response to
a question in a town meeting in Clinton, Massachusetts, used the
word "homeland" in referring to the Palestinians. At that March 16,
1977 meeting, the president said that an "ultimate requirement for
peace is to deal with the Palestinian problem. . . . There has to
be a homeland providing for the Palestinian refugees who have suffered for many, many years."[19]

The direct relationship between the Palestinian conflict and
U.S. national interests, economic and strategic, was repeated by
Harold Saunders as recently as November 1981. In a study prepared
as part of a project on U.S. vital interests in regions of conflict,
Saunders stated:

The Arab-Israeli conflict not only involves the United
States commitment to the security and future of
Israel but also engages the interests of countries
throughout the Middle East. The Palestinian cause
has even become an important symbol in North-South
relations. Active United States diplomacy in reducing
the causes of conflict and moving the conflict toward
resolution is critical to the pursuit of United States
interests throughout the Middle East and can even also
enhance the capacity of the United States to deal with
conflict elsewhere in the developing world.[20]

Saudi policy makers became optimistic that a U.S.-supported
peace initiative was underway, and Saudi policy pushed actively
toward that goal. Specifically, the Saudi government supported the
secretary of state's statement on September 30, 1976 at the United
Nations calling for the reconvening of the Geneva Peace Conference.[21] Saudi Arabia also endorsed the October 1, 1977 joint
U.S.-Soviet statement on the Middle East. The two superpowers
indicated an urgent need for "achieving, as soon as possible, a just
and lasting settlement of the Arab-Israeli conflict."[22]

Unfortunately, however, the optimism of 1976 and early 1977
regarding a breakthrough on the peace front dissipated since there
were no tangible results. The Geneva conference produced no substantive changes, the private contacts that were supposed to occur
between the United States and the Palestinian leadership did not
materialize, and as a result of strong pressure from Israel,

Soviet-U.S. cooperation on the Middle East did not progress. In addition, a rightist Likud government, under the leadership of Menachem Begin, came to power in Israel for the first time since 1948. This government was not inclined to negotiate the future of the West Bank and Gaza if such negotiations were to exclude a priori Israeli sovereignty in those territories. Indeed, the March 1977 Likud Party platform stated that the Jewish people have the right to the land of Israel (Erez Israel), which meant that Judea and Samaria (West Bank) would not be handed to any foreign adminis-tration; "between the sea and Jordan there will only be Israeli sovereignty."[23]

With the freezing of the Middle East situation and the seeming inability of the superpowers to generate any real progress, Presi-dent Sadat came to the realization that: any hope for peace in the Middle East resided in the conflicting parties themselves, not in outside powers; and if he did not act boldly and quickly, he would lose the diplomatic momentum that started with the October War four years earlier. Consequently, contrary to the advice of some of his advisers, he broke with his fellow Arabs and indicated his willingness to negotiate with Israel face to face. He delivered that message on his visit to Israel in November 1977, thus starting a period of personalized diplomacy that heralded the Camp David era.[24]

SAUDI PERCEPTIONS AND POLICIES, FALL 1977–SUMMER 1979

In spite of the continued significance of the Persian Gulf to the United States, the 1977–79 period was dominated by Sadat's initiative. Saudi policy on Palestine during this period was aligned with Arab diplomacy, which was critical of Sadat's quest for peace with Israel. On the other hand, Saudi Arabia showed some under-standing of Sadat's initiative and adopted a low-key approach toward the Egyptian leader. In essence Saudi leaders understood that Sadat wanted to regain the territory that traditional Arab diplomacy, both moderate and radical, had failed to gain. Secondly, the Saudis did not disapprove of Sadat's objective of urging the United States to become involved more actively. Finally, the Saudis generally supported the proposals of Sadat's speech to the Israeli Knesset (Parliament) on November 20, 1977. In that speech, President Sadat indicated that he did not seek a separate or a partial peace between Egypt and Israel, that peace must be based on justice, that occupation must be terminated, and that the legitimate rights of the Palestinian people must be recognized. Nor did Saudi Arabia

disagree with the essential elements of the peace that President
Sadat envisioned in his Jerusalem speech. Such a peace agreement,
according to President Sadat, should include the following points:

Ending the occupation of the Arab territories occupied since 1967.
Achievement of the fundamental rights of the Palestinian people and
their right to self-determination, including their right to establish their own state.
The right of all states in the area to live in peace within their
boundaries, which will be secured and guaranteed through procedures to be agreed upon, which will provide appropriate security to international boundaries in addition to appropriate international guarantees.
Commitment of all states in the region to administer their relations
in accordance with the objectives and principles of the United
Nations Charter, particularly the principle concerning resolving
their differences by peaceful means rather than by force.
Ending the state of belligerence in the region.[25]

The 1977-79 period primarily consists of three major developments: President Sadat's visit to Israel (November 20, 1977); the
signing of the Camp David Framework for Peace (September 17,
1978); and the signing of the Egyptian-Israeli Peace Treaty (March
26, 1979). Saudi Arabia, while disagreeing with the tactics of
President Sadat, did agree with the principles he advocated, both
in Israel and at Camp David. Like other Arab moderates, Saudi
leaders thought that Sadat underestimated Begin's intransigence,
particularly in dealing with the West Bank and with the Palestinians.
However, Saudi Arabia refrained from condemning President Sadat
publicly.

Saudi Arabia, for example, did not join the rejectionist front
("Steadfastness and Confrontation Front"), which was composed of
Libya, Algeria, Iraq, People's Democratic Republic of Yemen
(South Yemen), Syria, and the PLO. Nor did Saudi Arabia attend
the rejectionist Arab summit held in Libya on December 5, 1977
following Sadat's visit to Israel.[26]

Following the signing of the Camp David Framework on September 17, 1978, Saudi Arabia and several other Arab states attended a special summit in Baghdad, Iraq on November 2-5, 1978.
The assembled heads agreed to impose economic and political sanctions on Egypt if Sadat signed a separate peace agreement with Israel.
It was believed at the time that the Saudi presence acted as a moderating influence on the summit.

In a magazine interview following that meeting, Saudi Crown
Prince Fahd minimized the significance of the Saudi participation in

the Baghdad summit.[27] Although the Saudis were criticized by some
Arabs for their moderate position on Sadat's initiative, they continued to see some hope for a comprehensive, genuine peace through
the Camp David Framework. In that framework, the parties
pledged "to reach a just, comprehensive, and durable settlement
of the Middle East conflict through the conclusion of peace treaties
based on Security Council Resolutions 242 and 338 in all their
parts."[28] The Saudis believed that both Carter and Sadat were
genuinely committed to the goal of a just, comprehensive peace.
However, later events indicated that Prime Minister Begin did not
share that commitment.

The final blow for Saudi Arabia and the rest of the Arab states
was, of course, the signing of the separate Egyptian-Israeli Peace
Treaty on March 26, 1979, only six months after Camp David. Consequently, Saudi Arabia participated in the Arab League summit
held in Baghdad on March 27-31, 1979. The summit members decided, among other things, to withdraw Arab ambassadors from
Egypt and to move the headquarters of the Arab League from Cairo
to Tunis.[29]

SAUDI PERCEPTIONS AND POLICIES,
FALL 1979-PRESENT

Since the fall of 1979, there have been several important developments that directly relate to the connection between the Palestinian conflict and the Persian Gulf. Since these developments
occurred primarily in the gulf region, Saudi Arabia regained a
diplomatic initiative, which had been somewhat overshadowed by
Sadat's "shock" diplomacy of the preceding two years.

The first development stemmed from the Camp David Peace
Accords. By early 1980, it became clear to many observers that
the first part of the Camp David Framework, the Israeli-Egyptian
rapprochement, was working, and that both states were on schedule
in fulfilling their obligations under the agreement. It was equally
clear that the second part of the framework, the part dealing with
autonomy for the West Bank and Gaza, had not progressed.
Palestinians had not participated, the Begin government was not
forthcoming, Egypt was more concerned with its own internal affairs and with regaining the Sinai, and the United States was pre-
paring for the 1980 presidential election. The conclusion was that
there would be no further developments from the Camp David attempts for a just, comprehensive, and durable peace, and the
autonomy talks had deadened. The Arab world, as well as the rest
of the international community, had to accept that the Camp David
system was in reality reduced to a bilateral peace arrangement.

The second development was the collapse of the Shah and the rise of a chaotic, theocratic, revolutionary Islamic (Shi'ite) regime in Iran under the Ayatollah Rouhallah Khomeini. Apprehension quickly spread across the gulf to the family-centered regimes in Saudi Arabia and its neighbors. These regimes perceived a potentially serious threat from Khomeini's stated desire to export his Islamic revolution across the Gulf by Iranian nationals and/or the Shi'ite communities living on the Arab side of the gulf.[30] Of course, this included the eastern province of Saudi Arabia where the oil fields are located. Another ominous development was the Soviet invasion of Afghanistan. To the Saudis, the occupation of Afghanistan, the chaos in Iran, and the Iran-Iraq war were a sure formula for instability. In addition, many gulf leaders harbored doubts regarding U.S. resolve to respond adequately to another Soviet military threat if one should occur.[31] These gulf leaders were disillusioned with Washington's indecisive response to Khomeini regarding the U.S. hostages and to the Soviet invasion of Afghanistan.

When the United States began to seek closer military cooperation with gulf countries by acquiring basing and facilities rights, most of those countries were hesitant to identify openly with the United States. The reason given for this reluctance was the United States' continued support for Israel and Washington's inability to produce a settlement on the Palestinian conflict. In early 1980, most leaders in the region believed "that an American-induced Palestinian solution based on Palestinian self-determination would dramatically enhance America's prestige in the Islamic world, which in turn would serve American interests well."[32]

Assessing the emerging dichotomy between the need for U.S. military assistance and reluctance to identify openly with the United States and noting no progress in the autonomy negotiations, Saudi leaders began to take a leading Arab role in the search for a workable peace formula with Israel. What propelled Saudi leaders to actively seek a resolution of the conflict was the emerging belief that a resolution would serve Saudi national interests. To put it bluntly, they saw a Communist threat in the region, and they needed U.S. military cooperation. A resolution of the Palestinian conflict would make it much easier for the Saudis to conclude open military agreements with the United States, especially if Washington were to help produce such a settlement, even if it only recognized the minimal Palestinian demand for self-determination.

In a wide-ranging interview with Katharine Graham, chairperson of The Washington Post in May 1980, Crown Prince Fahd and Prince Abdulla, chief of the Saudi National Guard, indicated their willingness to accept the existence of Israel if it would terminate its occupation of the lands occupied since 1967 and recognize the principle of self-determination for the Palestinian people. The two Saudi leaders made the following points:

1. If Israel would declare its sincere intention of withdrawing from the lands occupied in 1967, Saudi Arabia would do its utmost to bring the Arabs to co-operate and work for a full settlement.
2. If the Palestinians get an entity of their own, then the other Arab states will help them develop their country and make it stable.
3. Communism and the Soviets are encircling the region. . . . Despite warnings from the highest author-ities in Saudi Arabia to the United States, there was no positive response when this was happening. . . .
4. The continuation of the present situation [Palestinian conflict] creates the climate most favorable to the spread of communism in the region. . . . Amer-ica has to convince Israeli leaders that war is not in their favor, not in the long run. The Americans through their military and economic aid should exercise pressure to show the Israelis this. [33]

In the period from the fall of 1980 through the spring of 1981, no tangible movement occurred toward peace. There was a resigned acceptance of the fact that not much could be done around the time of the U.S. presidential election and for a few months after the inaugu-ration. The defeat of Carter and the election of President Reagan also meant that the new administration required several extra months to reorder the government's priorities. Although foreign policy issues, particularly opposition to Soviet expansionism, helped elect President Reagan, he was preoccupied with the economy during the first year of his administration. Furthermore, in the Middle East itself, no progress was expected before the Israeli parliamentary elections in June 1981.

However, Persian Gulf leaders signaled the new administration as early as January 1981 that they desired a dialogue on issues of mutual concern. In a series of interviews conducted by the author in January 1981 with a number of gulf leaders and elite representatives, three points were frequently made.

1. They accepted the view that a commonality of Arab-U.S. interests exists in the Persian Gulf, but that questions of regional security, stability, and threats should ultimately be defined by the gulf states themselves. While they agreed with the United States' assessment of the potential Soviet threat to the gulf, they also viewed

Israel as a threat to the Arab world. However, Soviet occupation of Afghanistan was as abhorrent to them as Israeli occupation of Arab lands.

2. They generally believed that Palestine's problem could be quickly settled if Washington decided to pressure Israel into making concessions. They also believed that the pro-Israeli lobby in Washington "controls" U.S.-Mideast policy. Hence they were pessimistic about the possibility of any U.S. pressure on Israel.

3. They generally perceived a connection between the Palestinian conflict and regional security in the gulf. They believed that it is in the United States' interest to resolve the conflict, and they were therefore perplexed about why Washington did not vigorously pursue a settlement of the Palestinian conflict.

By early summer 1981, Saudi Arabia decided to offer its own peace proposal. At least four factors influenced the Saudis to assume a more active role: the failure of the Camp David Framework concerning the Palestinians; belief in the linkage between the Palestinian conflict and gulf security; the need to present a comprehensive, unified, negotiable position on the conflict; and, finally, a belief that the absence of a negotiated settlement would disturb Middle East stability and would pose a serious threat to the forces of moderation in the region. Frustration would lead to further violence, which could threaten the very existence of some Arab regimes, particularly in the Persian Gulf.

In response to this assessment, on August 7, 1981, Prince Fahd in a radio interview offered a peace plan based on the following principles:

Israel should withdraw from all Arab territory occupied in 1967, including Arab Jerusalem.

Israeli settlements built on Arab land after 1967 should be dismantled.

Freedom of worship should be guaranteed for all religions in the holy places.

There should be an affirmation of the right of the Palestinian people to return to their homes and a compensation for those who do not wish to return.

The West Bank and the Gaza Strip should have a transitional period, under the auspices of the United Nations, for a period not exceeding several months.

An independent Palestinian state should be set up with Jerusalem as its capital.

All states in the region should be able to live in peace.

The United Nations or member-states of the United Nations should guarantee to execute these principles.[34]

The fact that the plan was made at all was significant. What was also important was the oblique, albeit clear, in Middle Eastern political terminology, reference to Saudi acceptance of the existence of Israel (the seventh point).

The Saudi plan was a summary of the general Arab moderate position on the conflict. By late fall 1981, the plan was being given serious consideration by the Reagan administration, but when it came up for discussion at the November 1981 Arab summit in Fez, Morocco it was tabled, which was partially due to the opposition of radical Arab states. Of course, this was a setback to Saudi policy, but Saudi Arabia will probably continue to build a moderate Arab consensus on the conflict. In fact, Saudi Arabia could capitalize on Husni Mubarak's desire to reestablish contact with the moderate Arab states. Saudi diplomacy could be pivotal in convincing the Arab world to accept the new Egyptian president in spite of the Egyptian-Israeli Peace Treaty, provided that Egypt harden its position on Palestinian self-determination.

THE PALESTINIANS

In order to properly examine the resolution of the Palestinian conflict and its impact on gulf stability and on U.S. interests in that region, it would be useful to give a synoptic picture of the Palestinians. Until 1948, the vast majority of the Palestinians lived in Palestine. Between 1919 and 1946, the Arab people of Palestine constituted a large majority of the population, as shown in Table 4.1.

Since 1948, Palsstinians have scattered throughout the world, with a majority living in the Middle East as stateless persons, refugees, or citizens of other states. According to recent population estimates, Palestinians worldwide number over 4.25 million, with over 1.1 million in the West Bank and Gaza and over 600,000 in Israel (see Table 4.2).

The Palestinian population is mostly young and also highly educated. Several other comments should be made. Only 27 percent of the Palestinian people live in the West Bank and the Gaza Strip, which are the two areas occupied by Israel in 1967. This means that it would be extremely difficult for West Bank/Gaza leadership to engage in any peace negotiations without the PLO's approval and support. Second, about 15 percent of the Palestinians live in Israel, and despite the fact that at least 75 percent of them were born and raised in Israel, they have retained their Palestinian Arab cultural identity; while they might favor the establishment of a Palestinian state, a majority of them would prefer to stay where they are.

TABLE 4.1

Arabs and Jews in Palestine (1919-46)

	1919	1921	1931	1936	1946
Arab population	533,000	551,000	784,891	916,061	1,237,334
Jewish population	57,000	72,000	172,000	384,078	608,225
Total population	590,000	623,000	957,891	1,300,138	1,835,559
Percent Arab	90.3	88.4	82.0	70.5	64.9
Percent Jewish	9.7	11.6	18.0	29.5	35.1

Source: John Chapple, "Jewish Land Settlement in Palestine," in From Haven to Conquest, ed. Walid Khalidi (Beirut, Lebanon: Institute for Palestine Studies, 1971), p. 841.

Approximately half a million Palestinians live in the Persian Gulf region; the bulk of them reside in Kuwait. Indeed, Kuwait is the only gulf country in which there is a real Palestinian community. In the other gulf states, including Saudi Arabia, Palestinians hold varied positions, as teachers, oil technicians, and advisers to rulers. The families of thousands of Palestinians working in the gulf live in towns, villages, and refugee camps in the West Bank, Gaza and Jordan, and Lebanon.

The Palestine Liberation Organization is the only governmental structure that the Palestinians have. It was formed by the Arab League at the first Arab summit meeting in Alexandria, Egypt in 1964. It is an umbrella organization for the Palestinian movement and for all the major guerrilla organizations that comprise the movement. Since its foundation in 1964, the PLO has had three chairmen: Ahmad Shuqairi (1964 to late 1967); Yahya Hammouda (1968); and Yasser Arafat (early 1969 to present).

The decision to establish the PLO by the Arab League followed two earlier steps. The first step was recognition by the Arab League of the existence of a separate Palestinian entity (Kayan). The Arab League, under the influence of President Nasser of Egypt, encouraged Ahmad Shuqairi, a prominent pro-Egyptian Palestinian leader, to pursue the idea of a Palestinian "entity" with Palestinian leaders throughout the Arab world. At the first major assembly of representatives of the Palestinian people held in Jerusalem May 28–June 2, 1964), those assembled called on the Arab states to establish the Palestine Liberation Organization, whose constitution and national charter were adopted at that meeting.

TABLE 4.2

Palestinian Distribution throughout the World
(1981 estimates)

Country/Region	Total
West Bank (excluding East Jerusalem)	725,000
Gaza Strip	450,000
Israel (including East Jerusalem)	650,000
Jordan (East Bank)	1,150,000
Syria	200,000
Lebanon	350,000
Kuwait	300,000
Iraq	20,000
Libya	20,000
Egypt	50,000
Saudi Arabia	100,000
U.A.E., Qatar, and other gulf states	75,000
United States	100,000
Elsewhere	100,000
Total	4,290,000

Source: Compiled by the author.

The decision to establish the PLO responded to a growing unrest among Palestinian students and intellectuals over the inaction of Arab states on the question of Palestine. These states hoped that the PLO would contain this unrest and would also contain the rising militancy of such groups as Fateh (Movement for the Liberation of Palestine).

Between 1964 and 1967, the PLO was an organization of the Arab League and subject to the whims of Arab leaders. The first chairman of the PLO, Ahmad Shuqairi, made sure that Palestinian demands did not go beyond the policies of the Arab League. Accordingly, the first major Palestinian movement, Fateh, which came into being in the early 1960s and commenced its guerrilla military operations against Israel in January 1965, stayed out of the PLO. Fateh's leadership was strongly attacked by Arab regimes, and its top leader, Yasser Arafat, was arrested by Syrian authorities for about a month in 1964.

The situation changed radically after the June 1967 war, which resulted in the total defeat of Arab armies by Israel. Traditional Arab regimes were discredited, and the Palestine resistance movement acquired new credibility as the sole viable means of liberating Palestine.

Guerrilla control of the PLO was finalized at the fifth session of the Palestine National Congress in Cairo, February 2-4, 1969. That session was a turning point in the evolution of the Palestine Liberation Organization. The PLO was no longer an Arab League organization; it became a Palestinian organization—both in goals and administration. Yasser Arafat became the chairman of the PLO and chairman of the Executive Committee. This situation still holds true at the time of this writing.

However, since late 1977, the PLO has found itself in an increasingly difficult position. It had opposed the Camp David process, yet it was unable to divert President Sadat from his quest for peace with Israel or to force Prime Minister Begin to make any concessions in the occupied territories. The so-called Arab "rejectionist front" has been paralyzed as well. Ironically, the PLO is now at the mercy of Arab states, which is not very different from the situation that had prevailed in the late 1960s and early 1970s.

The PLO encompasses many organizations and movements and runs complex operations in Palestinian refugee camps, particularly in the areas of health, education, and welfare. The PLO's mainstream ideology reflects that of Fateh's: a bourgeois, nationalist program of action aiming at the establishment of an independent Palestinian political authority.

While Fateh is by no means the only organization within the PLO, it is the largest and the most influential. It also enjoys the support of most Arab states, particularly the moderates and the conservatives, as well as the Palestinian middle class of professionals, intellectuals, and businessmen. Fateh, which has the largest membership within the PLO's structure, has been headed by Yasser Arafat, since its inception in the early 1960s. By virtue of this position, he has also ascended to the chairmanship of the whole PLO organization. Other guerrilla organizations are: al-Asifah, Popular Front for the Liberation of Palestine (PFLP), Popular Front for the Liberation of Palestine-General Command,

Popular Democratic Front for the Liberation of Palestine (PDFLP), Sa'iqa, Arab Liberation Front, Popular Struggle Front, and Palestine Liberation Front. [35]

In terms of administration, the PLO consists of three bodies: the Palestine National Congress (PNC), the Central Council, and the Executive Committee. The Palestine National Congress is similar to a parliament in exile. It consists of about 300 representatives of Palestinians throughout the world. The PNC's membership also reflects the guerrilla groups within the PLO (on a prorated basis) and Palestinian popular organizations. Over 90 percent of the PNC's members hold a bachelor's degree, and over 15 percent hold a doctorate (Ph.D. or M.D.).

PNC has met roughly once a year in regular sessions since 1964, for a total of 15 regular sessions. Other than the first session, which was held in Jerusalem, and the third, held in Gaza (May 1966), most of the other sessions were held in Cairo. The fourteenth session (January 1979) and the fifteenth session (April 1981) were held in Damascus. Among the major decisions taken by the PNC over the years have been: adoption of a national charter; setting up Palestinian governmental institutions; rejection of U.N. Resolution 242; adoption of diplomacy as a vehicle for national liberation; a call for setting up a state on any part of Palestine liberated from Israel; rejection of the Camp David peace talks, and establishment of a new dialogue with Jordan.

The Central Council constitutes the second layer in PLO's bureaucracy. Established in 1973, it comprises about 55 members, including the Executive Committee, the chairman of the PNC, the commander of the Palestine Liberation Army (PLA), representatives of guerrilla organizations not represented in the Executive Committee, and a few independents. The Central Council, which acts as a liaison between the PNC and the Executive Committee, meets every three months and acts as a PNC in miniature.

The Executive Council is the closest to being a cabinet in exile. It is similar to a council of ministers in many countries. It consists of 15 members, each in charge of a certain department or function. Eight major departments are administered by the Executive Committee: military (including PLA); cultural and educational; political; Palestine National Fund; social affairs (including Palestine Red Crescent); occupied territories; popular and professional organizations; and information.

The Executive Committee, which is headed by Yasser Arafat, arrives at decisions collectively and after extended debate. Contrary to popular opinion, Arafat does not have complete decision-making power. The decision-making process within the PLO on any of the three levels is highly collective.

During the fifteenth session of the PNC, held in April 1981 in Damascus, PFLP rejoined the Executive Committee for the first time since 1974. The new Executive Committee consists of three representatives of Fateh, including Arafat as chairman, seven independents, one representative each from PFLP, PDFLP, Popular Front-General Command, Sa'iqa, and the Arab Liberation Front.

RESOLUTION OF THE PALESTINIAN CONFLICT:
IMPACT ON U.S. INTERESTS

Two opposing arguments have been advanced concerning the impact of the Palestinian conflict on U.S. interests in the Persian Gulf. The first maintains that the Arab/Islamic states of the Persian Gulf view the Palestinian question as central to peace and stability in the area. They have avoided being closely identified with the United States because of its continued support for Israel and for Israeli occupation of Arab lands, including East Jerusalem. Gulf leaders have often stated that if regional peace and stability are to endure, the Palestinian conflict, including Jerusalem, must be resolved. As long as this conflict continues, the United States cannot expect to establish long-range relations with the countries of the region; therefore U.S. strategic interests would remain in continual jeopardy.[36]

On the other hand, there is the argument that gulf instability is endemic, that gulf oil policies are to a large extent economic rather than political, that gulf regimes are very fragile, that a serious gap exists between the rulers and the people in those countries, and that the oil wealth and the concomitant modernization have created new sociocultural pressures in most gulf societies that are potentially threatening to internal stability and external security. Implicit in this argument is the assumption that the Palestinian question is basically tangential to U.S. strategic interests in the Persian Gulf, that with or without a solution regional stability will always be problematic, and that most of the primary factors contributing to this instability emanate from within the gulf itself.[37]

The argument that maintains that solving the Palestinian conflict is essential to U.S. strategic interests in the Persian Gulf rests on three basic supports. First, dependence on oil makes the gulf an integral part of U.S. national interest. Second, the cooperation of gulf governments, most of which are Arab and Islamic, is crucial for the United States in its endeavor to guard its national interest and in its efforts to repel any future Soviet aggression. Third, since Palestine is an important variable in their foreign policy, most gulf governments have made it amply clear to the United

States that they will not establish close relations with Washington until the administration resolves the Palestinian conflict.

The linkage between oil and Palestine is particularly significant in view of U.S. government oil projections, which indicate that any massive interruption of oil supplies from Persian Gulf countries would have a severe impact on the economies of the free world. In a testimony before the Senate Foreign Relations Committee in February 1980, John C. Sawhill, deputy secretary of energy, made the following additional points:

The vital role of the Persian Gulf in providing the free world with the oil it needs to maintain acceptable levels of economic growth will change little in the years ahead.

Total OECD (Organization for Economic Cooperation and Development) dependence on imported oil will not be significantly reduced before the mid-1980s.

Two-thirds of total free world oil reserves are located in the Persian Gulf area.

Persian Gulf countries produce about two-thirds of all oil in the world trade and about 40 percent of total free world oil output.

Because of their small populations, Persian Gulf countries consume only one-twentieth of the oil they produce, a situation that is not likely to change through the mid-1980s.[38]

U.S. policy makers became convinced of this linkage as early as the mid-1970s. Successive secretaries of state and other high government officials have often stated that solving the Arab-Israeli conflict serves the national interest of the United States. As early as September 1975, former Secretary of State Henry Kissinger stated that a settlement of the Arab-Israeli conflict was required to protect "the fundamental national interest of the United States," and that it was imperative that the United States have an active role in the pursuit of a settlement:

1. Because of our historical and moral commitment to the survival and well-being of Israel.

2. Because of our important interests in the Arab world—an area of more than 150 million people sitting astride the world's largest oil reserves.

3. Because the eruption of crisis in the Middle East would severely strain our relations with our allies in Europe and Japan.

4. Because continuing instability risks a new international crisis over oil and a new setback to the world's hopes for economic recovery threatening the

well-being not only of the industrial world, but of most
nations of the globe.

5. Because a crisis in the Middle East poses an
inevitable risk of direct United States-Soviet confrontation and has done so with increasing danger in every
crisis since the beginning.[39]

This position was reiterated by former Secretary of State
Vance: "The solution of the Arab-Israeli dispute is a key issue that
is necessary for the achievement of peace and stability in the region.
Therefore, one of the most important matters that we and others
have to devote our attention to is an effort to try and bring about a
satisfactory resolution of the Palestinian problem."[40]

Nor is this view restricted to the State Department. Early in
1980 editorials in the country's major newspapers also advocated a
vigorous U.S. approach to resolving the Palestinian conflict. To
illustrate, according to an editorial in the Miami Herald: "The
Palestinian question, of course, is the principal sore point between
the United States and the Islamic world. A solution is essential—
and now—or the whole Mideast peace plan so carefully woven at
Camp David may come unravelled."[41] "Movement on the Palestinian issue," wrote The Christian Science Monitor, "is essential
to stability in the Middle East."[42]

The resolution of the Arab-Israeli conflict has come to mean
a comprehensive resolution of the Palestinian conflict. To most,
if not all, Arab and Islamic states, an acceptable resolution must,
at the very minimum, comprise an Israeli withdrawal from the
occupied territories and a recognition of the legitimate national
rights of the Palestinians. The recognition of the Palestinians'
right to self-determination has become a major component of the
foreign policies of most Arab states, and, as indicated earlier, the
Saudi position has been very clear. In the words of Prince Saud
al-Faisal, Saudi Arabia's foreign minister, the Saudi position "is
based on the right of the Palestinians themselves to determine
whether they want an independent state, or an entity with links to
another country, or another solution.[43]

The necessity of resolving the Palestinian conflict and the
positive impact this would have on U.S. economic and strategic interests was amply illustrated in several recent congressional reports and hearings. In a report prepared by a congressional staff
study mission to the Persian Gulf and other countries, the point was
made that in the view of gulf leaders, the United States should produce a settlement of the Palestinian conflict that is acceptable to the
Palestinians. These leaders "regard a failure by the United States

to deal with the Palestinian problem as a harbinger for failure on the security side. . . ."[44]

In another report on the U.S.-Saudi special relationship, by by the Congressional Research Service, Saudi Arabia's importance to the United States was vividly highlighted, and accordingly U.S. strategic interests can best be served by continued U.S.-Saudi cooperation. The Saudi's special position, according to this study, derives from at least six factors:

It controls more than a quarter of the world's known deposits of petroleum;

It dominates geographically the Arabian Peninsula, borders both on Persian Gulf and the Red Sea, and lies on the southern flank of Israel's security zone;

Decisions by its leaders regarding the use of its huge financial reserves will continue to have a significant impact on the Western economic system;

As the dominant oil-producing and economic power in the Arabian Peninsula and as the center of the Islamic faith, it plays a key role in the maintenance of stability and security in the peninsula and the general areas of the Persian Gulf and the Red Sea;

It plays a key role—in recent years, a moderating one—in deliberations by OPEC; and

It is the seventh largest world market for United States goods, services, and technology, exclusive of arms sales.[45]

The above report further states that one of Saudi Arabia's major foreign policy objectives has been to seek "a comprehensive settlement of the Arab-Israeli conflict, including a resolution favorable to the Palestinians and Islamic interests in Jerusalem."[46] In spite of the crucial Saudi role in gulf stability and security, one of the factors that might cause problems in U.S.-Saudi future relations is the Saudi perception of the United States as being unable or unwilling to pressure Israel into a more moderate position on the Palestinian question.

The following statements, delivered at the congressional hearings, sum up the argument that resolving the Palestinian conflict is essential for the United States.

On March 24, 1980, Harold Saunders, the former assistant secretary of state for Near Eastern and South Asian affairs, declared:

We have long regarded the solution of the Arab-Israeli problem as central to stability in the area. . . . The nations in the gulf see continuing instability in the Arab-

Israeli area as playing back into their own security
situations . . . and [they] regard the resolution of
the Palestinian problem . . . as a contribution to
security in the gulf area. [47]

On May 5, 1980, William B. Quandt, the former National
Security Council official in charge of the Middle East, stated:

The Saudis very much want to be out of the position of
being under pressure from the Arabs to use oil as a
political weapon and under pressure from us not to do
so. The only way out, as they see it, is for the Palestinian issue to be on its way to a resolution, even though
they seem to be fairly realistic about how long that may
take. What they cannot tolerate over any long period of
time is the impression that the United States has given
up entirely on this issue. So some degree of credible
movement toward a solution of that issue is important
to them, at least as they see regional politics today. [48]

On July 28, 1980, Hermann Eilts, the ambassador to Saudi
Arabia and Egypt, said:

. . . if we are to solicit the cooperation of the Gulf
littoral states to meet the possible Soviet threat, it is
essential that a new climate of political confidence in
United States intentions vis-a-vis the Arab/Israeli
problem, be reestablished. [49]

Again, Harold Saunders, on September 2, 1980, noted:

The Palestinian issue weighs heavily on all the Gulf
governments and on our relations with them. . . .
Consistently these governments assert that absence
of peace in the Middle East is the primary threat to
Middle East security, including the stability of the
Gulf region. They regard tensions and alienations
created by a third of a century of conflict between
Arabs and Israelis as the main source of Soviet influence in the region, as a leading contributor to
revolution and radical political currents throughout
the Middle East, and as the primary obstacle to developing the sort of firm relationships with the United
States which their national interests otherwise call
for. [50]

Based on the statements above, a logical argument can be made for vigorous U.S. action toward a settlement based on self-determination. However, one question must be considered: What are the costs and benefits to the United States from such an action? Briefly stated, a strong U.S. move toward a comprehensive settlement would be applauded by most Arab/Islamic states, Third World countries, and Western Europe. The Soviet Union might also find it politically useful to support such a move, even though Moscow might be shut out of the process.

Gulf countries, particularly Saudi Arabia and perhaps Iraq, would see in this action a means to free themselves from the Palestinian burden. Also, they would feel more comfortable in dealing openly with the United States in gulf security matters. Many gulf leaders have already indicated, both publicly and in private, that they and Washington hold similar views on regional security, and that cooperation in this area could become a reality once they are no longer constrained by the Palestinian conflict.

Arab-U.S. trade and commerce would also benefit from a resolution of the conflict. Gulf countries would not hesitate to expand their economic relations with the United States, particularly in technology transfers, without being inhibited by such things as boycott by companies dealing with Israel.

In the political sphere, a U.S.-supported comprehensive and just settlement would introduce an element of stability into some of these countries. For example, Palestinians residing in the Persian Gulf would no longer be viewed as a threat. However, one must readily admit that internal stability is influenced by many more variables than the leaders' position on Palestine.

Of course, some authorities argue that solving the conflict would not necessarily enhance U.S. interests in the gulf. Regional stability, this argument maintains, is a function of many factors that fall outside the Palestinian conflict. They are demographic (small indigenous populations vs. large expatriate communities); religious (Shi'as vs. Sunnis); ideological (conservatives vs. leftists and monarchists vs. republicans); territorial (border disputes); economic (oil states vs. nonoil states); socioeconomic (rich vs. poor); political (authoritarian regimes vs. popular participation); and ethnic (Arab, Iranian, Kurdish, Baluchi, Alawite, Druze, Turkish, Jewish, etc.). The Iraq-Iran war is often cited in support of this argument.

Conflicts along these lines have gone on for centuries, have often been bloody, and certainly predate the state of Israel and the Arab-Israeli conflict. The displacement of Palestinians, this argument maintains, is only one factor in the myriad of Middle Eastern conflicts, and solving their case will only have a marginal effect on intrastate relations in the region.

Furthermore, solving the conflict will have no effect on OPEC's policies in terms of oil availability and pricing. As an economic organization, OPEC's policies have been largely influenced by market conditions. Decisions by OPEC members to raise the price of oil or to cut production, for example, have also been dictated by their desire to modernize, both economically and militarily. World inflation has also had its impact.

Since Persian Gulf security is linked to internal stability, unless gulf states address themselves to the potentially destabilizing domestic factors, internal stability will always remain in jeopardy. Among these factors are rapid modernization, religious fanaticism, autocratic tribal rule, and of course education, communications, and the advent of "alien" ideas.

On the regional level, many border disputes remain unsettled, and practically every gulf state is involved in one or more territorial disputes with its neighbors. Some states have yet to renounce their claims to other states' territory, and Iran still occupies three small gulf islands claimed by the United Arab Emirates. Cold war among the Arab states or between the Arab states and Iran, for example, is not a new phenomenon in the gulf. Nor is superpower rivalry in the Middle East as a whole. Therefore, according to this argument neither the domestic nor the regional variables that influence security and stability would be much affected by the resolution or continuance of the Palestinian conflict.

Moreover, U.S. dependence on gulf oil is not likely to diminish appreciably over the next several years, and only a drastic change in energy policy in the United States can change this trend. As long as the demand continues, the United States will be subject to policies of the oil-producing states.

Not withstanding this argument, the record clearly favors the position that resolving the conflict in a manner favorable to a majority of the Palestinians and to the mainstream Arab position would have a positive effect on regional stability. U.S. interests will be appreciably enhanced in a climate of stability and cooperation with the gulf states. Saudi Arabia, the United States' special partner in the gulf, would become a more dependable ally once Washington demonstrates a serious and genuine commitment to resolve the Palestinian conflict. The Saudis have made it amply clear that without a solution, stability cannot endure in the region, which means that continued access to Middle East oil is linked, directly or indirectly, to peace.

Consequently, one can only conclude that resolving the Palestinian conflict would have a positive impact on U.S. strategic interests in the gulf, that Washington should pursue a settlement with resolve, leadership, and vigor, and that Arab-U.S. relations would be greatly enhanced by a resolution of the conflict. While one cannot argue that the energy crisis will somehow dissipate or that oil prices will somehow fall as a result of a resolution, it is safe to state that a peaceful environment would be more conducive to economic cooperation. Finally, a resolution of the Palestinian conflict will not accomplish miracles, but it will help.

NOTES

1. The Search for Peace in the Middle East: Documents and Statements, 1967-79. Report prepared for the Subcommittee on Europe and the Middle East of the Committee on Foreign Affairs, House of Representatives by the Foreign Affairs and National Defense Division, Congressional Research Service, Library of Congress (Washington, D.C.: U.S. Government Printing Office, 1979), p. 269.

2. Ibid., p. 93.

3. Ibid., p. 270.

4. U.S. Interests in and Policy toward the Persian Gulf. Hearings before the Subcommittee on the Near East of the Committee on Foreign Affairs, House of Representatives, 92nd Cong., 2nd sess. (Washington, D.C.: U.S. Government Printing Office, 1972), p. 82.

5. Search for Peace, p. 272.

6. Emile A. Nakhleh, Arab-American Relations in the Persian Gulf (Washington, D.C.: American Enterprise Institute, 1975), p. 2.

7. Search for Peace, p. 1.

8. Ibid., p. 2.

9. Ibid., p. 3.

10. Ibid., p. 97.

11. The Persian Gulf, 1974: Money, Politics, Arms and Power. Hearings before the Subcommittee on the Near East and South Asia of the Committee on Foreign Affairs, House of Representatives, 93rd Cong., 2nd sess. (Washington, D.C.: U.S. Government Printing Office, 1975), pp. 258-59.

12. Ibid., pp. 5-14.

13. Search for Peace, p. 242.

14. Ibid., p. 273.

15. Ibid., p. 100.

16. Ibid., p. 101.

17. Ibid., p. 102.

18. The Palestinian Issue in Middle East Peace Efforts. Hearings before the Special Subcommittee on Investigations of the Com-

mittee on International Relations, House of Representatives, 94th Cong., 1st sess. (Washington, D.C.: U.S. Government Printing Office, 1976), p. 178; Search for Peace, p. 305.

19. Search for Peace, p. 311.

20. Harold H. Saunders, The Middle East Problem in the 1980s (Washington, D.C.: American Enterprise Institute, 1981), p. 82.

21. Search for Peace, p. 158.

22. Ibid., p. 159.

23. Ibid., p. 201.

24. Ibid., p. 224.

25. Ibid., p. 227.

26. Ibid., pp. 274-76.

27. Ibid., p. 277.

28. Ibid., p. 21.

29. Ibid., pp. 278-81.

30. "Islamic Revolution: Dangerous Export," Washington Post, October 22, 1979, p. A21.

31. "Securing the Gulf," New York Times, January 8, 1980, p. A19.

32. Ibid.

33. "Saudis Vow Aid on Accord If Israel Pledges Pullback," Washington Post, May 25, 1980, pp. A1, A22.

34. FBIS 5 (August 10, 1981):C4-C5.

35. The Middle East and North Africa, 1981-82, 28th ed. (London: Europa Publications, 1981), p. 89.

36. William J. Baroody, Sr., "What a Palestinian Solution Will Solve," Washington Post, November 7, 1979, p. A19; Emile A. Nakhleh, "The Palestine Conflict and U.S. Strategic Interests in the Persian Gulf," Parameters (March 1981):71-78.

37. Irving Kristol, "What a Palestine Solution Won't Solve," Washington Post, October 25, 1979, p. A21.

38. Testimony of John C. Sawhill, deputy secretary, Department of Energy, before the Senate Foreign Relations Committee, February 20, 1980, pp. 2-3, unpublished. The OECD countries include 19 industrial European nations, the United States, Canada, Japan, Australia, and New Zealand.

39. U.S. Policy in the Middle East: November 1974-February 1976, Selected Documents, no. 4 (Washington, D.C.: U.S. Government Printing Office, 1976), p. 10.

40. New York Times, January 16, 1980, p. A14.

41. "Autonomy for Palestinians Key to U.S.-Israel Relations," Miami Herald, February 13, 1980, p. A6.

42. Daniel Southerland, "Carter Initiative Faces Difficulties," Washington Post, October 5, 1979, p. A5.

43. Jim Hoagland, "Saud Politely Disagrees on Palestinians," Washington Post, October 5, 1979, p. A5.

44. U.S. Security Interests in the Persian Gulf. Report of a Staff Study Mission to the Persian Gulf, Middle East, and Horn of Africa, October 21-November 13, 1980 to the Committee on Foreign Affairs, House of Representatives (Washington, D.C.: U.S. Government Printing Office, 1981), p. 7.

45. Saudi Arabia and the United States: The New Context in an Evolving "Special Relationship." Report prepared for the Subcommittee on Europe and the Middle East of the Committee on Foreign Affairs, House of Representatives (Washington, D.C.: U.S. Government Printing Office, 1981), p. 1X.

46. Ibid., p. x.

47. U.S. Interests in, and Policies toward, the Persian Gulf, 1980. Hearings before the Subcommittee on Europe and the Middle East of the Committee on Foreign Affairs, House of Representatives, 96th Cong., 2nd sess. (Washington, D.C.: U.S. Government Printing Office, 1980), p. 53.

48. Ibid., pp. 136-37.

49. Ibid., p. 299.

50. Ibid., pp. 352-53.

5

U.S. POLICY
IN THE GULF

EVOLUTION OF POLICY PRIOR TO 1972

The United States has had an interest in the Persian Gulf/
Arabian Peninsula region since World War II. Relations with the
region have been multifaceted, however; the focus of these relations
has been on oil, the Arab-Israeli conflict, and containment of Soviet
expansionism. These issues are interrelated, and it is in the context of this triangular linkage that U.S. policy in the Persian Gulf
will be examined in this chapter. These three issues have been con-
stant factors in United States-Persian Gulf relations, but the intensity has varied depending on the crisis, the period, the location,
and the causes. The changes in events that have affected the three
issues since the 1940s have not detracted from their significance,
nor have they undermined the basic linkage between them.

In the area of oil, for example, the dependence of the industrial world on Middle Eastern oil has increased significantly, thereby making that region very pivotal in the economic well-being of the
Western world and Japan. The industrial world has become more
vulnerable than ever due to the advent of political independence for
these countries, the transfer of ownership of the oil industry from
private companies to the producing countries, the rise in the price
of oil, the concomitant accumulation of petrodollars in their coffers,
and the absence of an effective energy policy in the consuming countries. Since the United States has increased its oil imports, it has
also become more dependent on the region for energy. Washington
cannot afford to ignore regional developments, whether internal or
international in nature.

Likewise, the Arab-Israeli conflict underwent a transformation from Israel versus the Arab states to Israelis versus Palestinians. However, this transformation, which has also involved a merger of politics and oil, has affected neither the validity nor the inevitability of the linkages. On the contrary, the four Arab-Israeli wars since 1948, particularly the 1973 war, have intertwined the three issues and have even forced the United States to be a conscious and active partner in the process of conflict resolution. Furthermore, since 1975 the United States has come to accept the emerging Arab thesis that the Palestinian question is central to the resolution of the Arab-Israeli conflict.

The third side of the triangle, containment of Soviet expansion in the Middle East, has also occupied the United States since the late 1940s. This was part of a worldwide policy of containment against the spread of international communism. A cardinal tenet of U.S. foreign policy has been to keep the Middle East and more recently the Persian Gulf free from Soviet control, either by proxy or directly. U.S. policy from the Truman Doctrine to the Carter Doctrine amply illustrates Washington's persistent perception of the threat of Soviet expansion.

Between 1948 and 1968, the United States treated the gulf as a British domain and relied on the British military and political presence to maintain the region "east of Suez" relatively stable and free of Soviet influence. During that 20-year period, the gulf was only tangential to the Arab-Israeli dispute. Oil, which was produced, refined, and marketed by oil corporations, was available in unlimited quantities at very low prices. Furthermore, it was not until the early 1970s that U.S. demand for imported oil began to take a critical upward swing.

During that same period, military agreements concerning U.S. naval facilities were concluded between the United States and Britain. The agreement to provide homeporting facilities in Bahrain for the U.S. minifleet, Command Middle East Force (COMIDEASTFOR), was an example. After Bahrain became independent in 1971, the facilities agreement was concluded between the United States and Bahrain directly. Indeed, COMIDEASTFOR was the vehicle through which a continuing U.S. naval presence was provided in the gulf in this period. Other defense-related arrangements in the 1950s and 1960s were pursued by the United States in the context of regional collective security agreements, such as the Baghdad Pact/CENTO, as well as through bilateral agreements with Iran, Iraq, and Saudi Arabia.

Washington's policy of containment in the 1950s was to maintain a pro-Western, stable Iran, which meant a Pahlavi regime, and to encourage Saudi Arabia and Iraq to emerge as a conservative,

Islamic force. This force would counteract the rising tide of Arab nationalism and Third World national liberation movements under the leadership of President Nasser of Egypt and other Third World leaders. The U.S. government, particularly Secretary of State John Foster Dulles, viewed these movements as unfriendly to the West and therefore, by definition, a fertile environment for Soviet ideological expansionism.

With the 1958 revolution and the toppling of the pro-Western monarchy, Iraq pulled out of the Baghdad Pact. Over the next 20 years, it completely swung from a pro-Western position to close friendship with the Soviet Union. Iran and Saudi Arabia became the only two pillars of stability in the U.S. and Western edifice of gulf security. This Iranian role, under the leadership of the Shah, reached its zenith with the Nixon Doctrine in the 1969-72 period. This "twin pillar" diplomacy, which lasted for about a decade, collapsed with the downfall of the Shah in late 1978 and early 1979. Once the United States adjusted to the loss of Iran's support, it began to strengthen the Saudi pillar, a policy that assumed heightened urgency following the Soviet invasion of Afghanistan.

Although the energy crisis did not penetrate the psyche of the U.S. public until the early 1970s, and even then very reluctantly, the U.S. government was well aware of the long-term need for imported oil and the corresponding long-term significance of the Persian Gulf. However, official awareness of the impending energy crisis was not translated into a public energy policy because of the government's complacency, its false sense of security and independence, a strong lobbying effort by the oil industry, an abundance of cheap oil, and an expanding national economy.

The evolution of U.S. policy in the gulf may be divided into two distinct stages: 1947 to 1972 and 1972 to the present. In the pre-1972 period, Washington's Persian Gulf policy was part of a general Middle East policy. However, several official statements by government officials referred specifically to the gulf. One of the early references in the post-World War II era to the significance of Middle East oil to U.S. national interest was made in 1947-48 by James Forrestal, the first U.S. secretary of defense. A synopsis of Forrestal's views on the subject as recorded in his diaries follows:

> I said that Middle East oil was going to be necessary
> for this country not merely in wartime but in peace-
> time, because if we are going to make the contribution
> that it seems we have to make to the rest of the world
> in manufactured goods, we shall probably need very
> greatly increased supplies of fuel.[1]

I took the position that because of the rapid depletion
of American oil reserves and an equally rising curve
of consumption we would have to develop resources
outside the country. The greatest field of untapped oil
in the world is in the Middle East.[2]

Without access to Middle Eastern pools . . . we could
not fight a war and we could not even maintain the
tempo of our peacetime economy, [and] we would have
to convert "within ten years" to four-cylinder cars.[3]

It is doubtful if there is any segment of our foreign relations of greater importance or of greater danger in
its broad implications to the security of the United
States than our relations in the Middle East.[4]

Forrestal argued very strongly that U.S. strategic interests
and the Palestinian conflict were linked: "And the Palestine issue,
of course, intimately involved our relations with the Middle East
and its oil supplies."[5] He further argued that in view of U.S. long-
term strategic interests in the Middle East, it was "stupid" to cause
"permanent injury to our relations with the Moslem world or to
stumble into war."[6]

Every U.S. president since World War II in one way or another has underscored the importance of the Persian Gulf to the
United States, both economically (oil) and strategically (against
Soviet expansion). Aside from their involvement in and concern
about problems in Fertile Crescent countries, Presidents Dwight
Eisenhower and John Kennedy focused primarily on Iran. Eisenhower was involved in the Mossadegh crisis and the reestablishment of the Shah's position as ruler of Iran.[7] President Kennedy
was only briefly concerned with Iran and then only as part of the
United States' effort to contain the Soviet Union.[8] But he also became indirectly involved with the Saudis as a result of the Egyptian
military involvement in Yemen in 1962 in support of the republicans
(which President Kennedy recognized) and against the royalists
(which the Saudis supported).[9]

The two major issues that occupied President Lyndon Johnson
were Vietnam in foreign policy and the building of the "Great Society"
domestically. The Middle East was thrust upon President Johnson
in 1967 with the June war. Therefore most references in the public
papers of President Johnson are to the third Arab-Israeli war and
the United States and United Nations efforts to work out the compromise that resulted in Security Council Resolution 242.[10] When he
referred to Iran on official occasions, as in the official welcoming

remarks to the Shah in August 1967, the president concentrated on internal socioeconomic progress in Iran, with almost no mention of the gulf region.[11]

President Richard Nixon assumed office in January 1969 with a world view totally different from that of his predecessor. Whereas Johnson was preoccupied with Vietnam and with advocating that cause, Nixon, with the insights of his national security advisor, Henry Kissinger, began to seek ways to extricate the United States from Vietnam. Slowly but surely, President Nixon began to direct his interest toward the Persian Gulf, even though he was also involved in the search for new initiatives to resolve the Arab-Israeli conflict and to reduce tensions on the Israeli-Egyptian border.[12]

By mid-1970, President Nixon began to view the Middle East from a larger perspective than just the Arab-Israeli conflict. In a conversation with the press on foreign policy on July 1, 1970, Nixon remarked: "The Mideast is important. We all know that 80 percent of Europe's oil and 90 percent of Japan's oil comes from the Mideast."[13] At the same meeting, he also stated that "the situation in the Mideast is more dangerous [than Vietnam] because it involves . . . a collision of the superpowers."[14]

President Nixon issued four major annual reports to Congress on foreign policy: February 18, 1970; February 25, 1971, February 9, 1972; and May 3, 1973. In all of them the president focused on the importance of a lasting peace in the region. The point of emphasis was that such a peace must be related to the balance of power in the region and secondly to a U.S.-Soviet understanding that the superpowers should help preserve the peace by discouraging any arms race in the area. While recognizing that "the greatest threat to peace and stability in the Middle East remains the Arab-Israeli conflict," President Nixon added that a "secure peace in the Middle East requires stable relations on both levels—accommodation within the region and a balance among the powers outside."[15]

President Nixon's first reference to the Persian Gulf appeared in his third report on February 9, 1972, but it was no more than an aside: "In the Persian Gulf, the special treaty relationships between Britain and some of the sheikhdoms ended in 1971; the stability of new political entities and structures remains to be consolidated."[16] In the fourth report (May 3, 1973), which followed the 1972 National Security Study Memorandum on the Middle East, the president's references to the Persian Gulf were positive in that he praised the newly independent lower gulf states for their efforts to cooperate with each other and for assuming responsibility for their own security. He indicated that Iran and Saudi Arabia had "undertaken greater responsibility for helping to enhance the area's stability. . . ."[17] He also stated that as United States' and other industrial nations' energy

demands rose, the need for Persian Gulf oil would increase. Therefore "assurance of the continuing flow of Middle East energy resources is increasingly important for the United States, Western
Europe and Japan."[18]

EVOLUTION OF POLICY SINCE 1972

In 1972 Washington concluded a major review of its interests
and policy options in the Persian Gulf. The review was prompted
by several factors: the British withdrawal from the region (which
was announced in 1968 and completed in 1971); the increasing dependence of the industrial world on gulf oil; the formation of newly independent small states in the lower gulf; and the threat that leftist
and reform-oriented movements posed to the tribal regimes in the
new states. Other reasons contributing to the review were: the
Nixon Doctrine; the post-Vietnam desire on the part of the United
States to have local leaders participate in the defense of their security with U.S. support but without U.S. troops; and the U.S.-Soviet
détente.

The review was contained in an internal National Security
Study Memorandum (NSSM 238), which as of this writing remains
classified. It is believed that the principles included in that document have governed Washington's Persian Gulf policy since 1972.
A summary of those broad principles was given by Joseph Sisco,
the former assistant secretary of state for Near Eastern and South
Asian affairs, in testimony to a congressional committee on August
8, 1972.

Noninterference in the internal affairs of other nations;
Encouragement of regional cooperation for peace and progress;
Supporting friendly countries in their efforts to provide for their
own security and development;
The principles enunciated at the Moscow Summit of avoiding con-
frontations in such areas in the world; and
Encouraging the international exchange of goods, services, and
technology.[19]

In applying these broad principles to the Persian Gulf, Sisco
stated that Washington's interests and policies toward the gulf would
include the following steps:

Support "orderly political development . . . and regional cooperation to assure the tranquility and progress of the area."[20]

Support local governments "in maintaining their independence and
assuring peace, progress, and regional cooperation without our
interfering in the domestic affairs of these friendly countries."[21]

Encourage "Iran, Saudi Arabia, Kuwait, and the smaller states to
cooperate wholeheartedly with one another to assure that the region remains secure."[22]

Assist "in the modernization of the Armed Forces of Iran and Saudi
Arabia to enable them to provide effectively for their own security
and to foster the security of the region as a whole."[23]

Extend Washington's "diplomatic presence into the area."[24]

Continue to maintain "a small American naval contingent at Bahrain
which has for a quarter century carried out the mission of visit-
ing friendly ports in the region to symbolize American interest."[25]

During that same congressional hearing, Sisco summarized the
rising importance of the Persian Gulf to U.S. national interests,
strategically and economically. "What we are after here is stability,
the kind of a climate in which peaceful and friendly relations can be
maintained between the United States and a number of these countries, so that we have equal opportunities economically and we have
this area available in terms of communications and transit."[26]

The principles enunciated in NSSM 238 of 1972 have remained
for the most part the basis of U.S. policy toward the Persian Gulf/
Arabian Peninsula/Indian Ocean region for a decade. Such developments as the 1973 October War, the rise in the price of oil, the collapse of the Shah, and the Soviet invasion of Afghanistan have often
frustrated implementation of some of the principles defined above.
But the principles have remained; indeed diligent pursuit of these
principles has compelled the United States to become more directly
involved in the politics of the gulf region—politically, economically,
and strategically. To U.S. leaders since 1973, the search for an
Arab-Israeli peace on the western side of Arabia has been a logical
extension of, even a prerequisite for, a closer Arab-U.S. partnership on the eastern periphery of the peninsula.

Although there were few references to the Persian Gulf in
statements by U.S. presidents and other high government officials
in the pre-1972 period, the record since 1972 is replete with policy
statements and agreements between the United States and gulf countries. Furthermore, an examination of the record indicates that,
beginning in late 1973, a triangular relationship evolved during the
period from 1973 to 1980 under three presidents in the context of
four major issues relating to the Middle East and the Persian Gulf:
the October War and the oil embargo (which occupied the attention
of President Nixon from 1973 to 1974); the disengagement agreements (which concerned President Ford from 1974 to 1975); the Camp

David Accords and the Egyptian-Israeli peace process (which involved President Carter from 1977 to 1979); and the collapse of Iran, the holding of the U.S. hostages, and the Soviet invasion of Afghanistan (which also preoccupied President Carter from 1979 to 1980).[27]

The most cursory review of presidential statements in the period between President Nixon's first State of the Union Message in January 1969 and President Carter's last in January 1980 amply illustrates the dramatic transformation in United States' perceptions of the Persian Gulf and policies toward it. The transformation went from Nixon's benign praise of the Shah's social "white revolution" in Iran to Carter's declaration of the gulf a part of Washington's vital interests. In military terms, the U.S. connection moved from a three-ship Command Middle East Force fleet, whose task was to show the U.S. flag on friendly missions, to a Rapid Deployment Force of 100,000 troops, whose task (as can be best defined) would be to repel any serious threat to gulf security. The economic picture illustrates the staggering nature of this transformation even more graphically.

The three-way linkage and United States' concern for Persian Gulf stability since 1972 have been prevalent themes not only in presidential statements but also in practically every congressional hearing and in every official statement on the Middle East from either the Department of State or the Department of Defense. Beginning in 1973, these statements even began to list the Arabian Peninsula/Persian Gulf area separately from the rest of the Middle East. This, of course, highlighted the importance of the peninsula and the gulf in regional peace and security and in Washington's long-term policy planning.

A year after Assistant Secretary of State Joseph J. Sisco enunciated the broad principles that would guide U.S. policy in the gulf, he returned to Congress to testify on the United States' position on the Arab-Israeli conflict and the Arabian Peninsula-Persian Gulf area. In a testimony before the Subcommittee on the Near East and South Asia of the House of Representatives, Sisco enumerated four United States objectives in the gulf:

1. Support for indigenous regional collective security efforts to provide stability and to foster orderly development without outside interference. . . .

2. Peaceful resolution of territorial and other disputes among the regional states and the opening up of better channels of communication among them.

3. Continued access to Gulf oil supplies at reasonable prices and in sufficient quantities. . . .

4. Enhancing of our commercial and financial interests.[28]

The four policy objectives were repeated a year later by Sisco's successor, Alfred L. Atherton, Jr., assistant secretary of state for Near Eastern and South Asian affairs, in his testimony to Congress. However, because of the accumulation of enormous oil-generated wealth in the hands of oil producers, Atherton added a fifth objective: "to assist and encourage the countries of the region to recycle their surplus revenues into the world economy in an orderly and undisruptive manner."[29] These five objectives combined in 1974-75 to produce the establishment of joint commissions on the economic and security fields between the United States, Saudi Arabia, and Iran, as well as closer Saudi-Iranian cooperation, also in the economic and security fields. The first result came to be called the conduct of foreign policy by joint commission, while the other became known as the "twin pillar" diplomacy.

However, the changes that occurred in the Persian Gulf in 1974, such as the lifting of the oil embargo, the vast increase in oil revenues, the change in the agreements of the oil companies with the producing states, and the expressed desire of gulf states for economic, technical, and technological cooperation with the United States, urgently indicated the need for a more clearly defined U.S. policy. Critical questions were posed in reference to the new realities in the region and to the need for new policies. To illustrate, Congressman Lee H. Hamilton, chairman of the Subcommittee on the Near East and South Asia, identified four examples of the changes that were rapidly occurring in the gulf and raised several questions pertaining to each of the four examples.

> First, it is amply clear that increased Iranian-Saudi Arabian cooperation in strategic, political and economic spheres is vital to maintaining our interests in this region in the future. Do our military supplies and other policies promote trust and confidence in regional cooperation? How are we encouraging Iran to cooperate with Saudi Arabia?
>
> Second, it is clear that United States oil companies in the region are being forced toward a new type of relationship with the producing states. . . . What role does the United States Government plan on playing in future negotiations with producing states? What is the United States doing to try to bring the oil prices down?
>
> Third, an enormous amount of money is accumulating in the Persian Gulf. . . . What policies is our Government developing to deal with this new financial world? How are we trying to recycle petrodollars? What advice are we giving United States companies?

Fourth, it is also clear that, while the challenge
of evolving effective policies toward the large states of
the region . . . will be a major policy dilemma for the
coming years, the United States faces another type of
challenge in developing policy strategies toward the
smaller states of the area. . . .[30]

Those were certainly important questions, but not one of them
touched on the interests, concerns, plans, and aspirations of the
local states themselves. While Congressman Hamilton's questions
helped set the stage for foreign policy planning toward the gulf, they
also prepared the ground for many disagreements between the United
States and its friends in the region.

The five policy objectives of the United States in the Arabian
Peninsula/Persian Gulf area that were enumerated by Assistant Secretary of State Atherton in August 1974 were restated approvingly
by Under Secretary of State for Political Affairs Joseph J. Sisco
in a congressional hearing on June 10, 1975.[31] Sisco indicated that
in view of these objectives, United States' policy toward the gulf's
four political entities (Iran, Saudi Arabia, Kuwait, and the lower
gulf states) has been designed to combine arms sales to these countries with the overall policy objectives of the United States. Such a
policy is basically a response to their own policy goals. These
states have, according to Sisco, expressed concerns in the political,
economic, cultural, and defense fields, and they have sought cooperation with the United States. Therefore Under Secretary Sisco argued that "given our mutuality of interests, it is reasonable and
sensible for us to support the policy goals of these friendly countries, where such goals parallel our own."[32] This approach governed the making of U.S. policy toward the gulf for the remainder
of the 1970s.

By the 1980s, the policy principles of the previous decade became somewhat inadequate. Those states that became independent
in 1971 had developed relatively stable regimes and polities, and
for the most part, they did manage to settle their territorial disputes peacefully (with the exception of Iran and Iraq). The United
Arab Emirates survived the decade as a federated state, with signs
of even more stability for the future; six gulf Arab states, including
Saudi Arabia but excluding Iraq, formed the Gulf Cooperation Council, a new and potentially far-reaching arrangement.

In terms of recycling petrodollars, Persian Gulf states have
pursued sophisticated and responsible monetary policies that have
benefited them as well as the industrial countries, and practically
all of these policies have well-conceived, albeit ambitious, economic, social, and educational developmental plans. Since the

termination of the oil embargo in the spring of 1974, OPEC's policies have been largely governed by economic, rather than political, considerations and, under the leadership of Saudi Arabia, have not been irresponsible.

On the negative side, the advent of the 1980s marked a continuation of the Palestinian conflict and Israeli occupation of Arab lands, a persistence of chaos in Iran, a tenacious Soviet occupation of Afghanistan, and a destructive border war between Iran and Iraq. U.S. foreign policy makers began to reorder their policy objectives toward the gulf to take Soviet expansionism into consideration. The new decade began with President Carter's response to the Soviet invasion of Afghanistan, stating, among other things, that resisting Soviet expansionism had become a major policy goal of the United States. This theme permeated official pronouncements on U.S. policy in the gulf throughout the year. In an address before the Council on Foreign Relations in March 1980, Secretary of Defense Harold Brown identified Washington's interests in the Persian Gulf as follows: to insure access to adequate oil supplies; to resist Soviet expansion; to promote stability in the region; and to advance the Middle East peace process, while insuring the continued security of Israel.[33]

In September 1980, Assistant Secretary of State for Near Eastern and South Asian Affairs Harold H. Saunders indicated in a congressional hearing that U.S. interests in the gulf since the early 1970s "have changed little in nature but have grown in importance."[34] In pursuing these "longstanding, major and interrelated"[35] interests, the United States takes notice of the following factors:

1. the area's strategic location and its significance to maintaining a global strategic balance;
2. the significance we place on the sovereignty and independence of these countries as part of a more stable world;
3. the world's vital need for the region's oil; and
4. the importance of these states in international finance and development and as markets for our goods and technology.[36]

The Reagan administration's attitude toward the Persian Gulf during its first year in office was heavily influenced by the Soviet presence in Afghanistan and by perceived Soviet threats throughout the region. In a statement before the Senate Foreign Relations Committee on September 17, 1981, Secretary of State Alexander Haig indicated that the U.S. strategy in the Middle East must be to "protect our vital interests in an unstable area exposed not only to historic Arab-Israeli rivalries but increasingly to threats from the

Soviet Union and its proxies."[37] In Haig's view, ultimate regional
security can be maintained through a system of security agreements
between the United States and the major states of the region (Egypt,
Israel, and Saudi Arabia). Such an "arc of strategic consensus" is
based on the premise that "intimate connections" exist between the
Middle East/Persian Gulf region and adjacent areas and that instability in one area will adversely affect the other areas in the region.[38]

Two weeks later, in another statement before the Senate Foreign
Relations Committee, Secretary Haig defended the sale of AWACS
(Airborne Warning and Control Systems) to Saudi Arabia on the grounds
that the deal would in the end serve U.S. interests. He identified four
elements in U.S. strategy in the gulf region:

> 1. improving our own military position in and
> near the region;
> 2. strengthening the defense capabilities of our
> friends;
> 3. restoring confidence in the United States as a
> reliable partner; and
> 4. pursuing a permanent peace in the region.[39]

Since the early 1970s, Washington has concluded numerous
treaties and agreements with gulf countries in pursuit of the policy
objectives that evolved during that period. These agreements cover
a vast array of areas: economic, military, technical, cultural, and
commercial. Some of these agreements will be examined in the following section.

TREATIES AND AGREEMENTS

In pursuing its policy objectives in the Persian Gulf, the
United States has concluded several major agreements with gulf
states since the early 1970s. These agreements have covered a
wide range of topics: defense, Peace Corps, agricultural com-
modities, atomic energy, aviation, education, economic and technical cooperation, environmental cooperation, trade and commerce,
publications, visas, judicial assistance, postal matters, telecom-
munications, investment guarantees, desalination, military missions, and even extradition.[40] Several comments are pertinent to
these treaties and agreements:

First, because of their size and importance, the majority of
these treaties have been with Saudi Arabia and Iran. Since the establishment of the Islamic Republic, most of the treaties with Iran

have been barely operative, but U.S. agreements with Saudi Arabia have been numerous and active.

Second, the common features of most of these agreements are military, economic, and technical assistance. This fact seems to reflect a consensus between Washington and the states involved on the need for closer economic cooperation and for improved defense in the region.

Third, like other policy approaches, U.S. diplomacy by treaty reflects an awareness of the significance of the gulf as a source of oil for the Western world, as an enormous source of capital, as a vast market for Western products and expertise, and as an area possibly coveted by the Soviet Union and other potentially anti-Western political movements. Therefore, U.S. policy makers have consistently attempted to tie the Persian Gulf to the United States and to the West in general, both economically and militarily, as the best guarantee of regional stability.

Fourth, most of these treaties seem to be a logical response to mutual needs: a need for recycling the so-called "Arab petrodollars" through Western financial institutions, and an Arab need for Western technology, arms, and managerial expertise. Gulf elites have stated on many occasions that while they disagree with Washington's policy on the Palestinian conflict, they admire U.S. technology, management techniques, corporate efficiency, and educational and technical training. Gulf leaders have also turned to the United States to build and modernize their defenses. The gulf has become almost a captive market for and a primary importer of United States' weapons systems. Oil and arms have become inextricably linked.

Fifth, as Table 5.1 indicates, the U.S. defense agreements with gulf countries have followed a pattern that has reflected a number of developments: (1) the application of the Nixon Doctrine, 1969-73, to the gulf through Iran; (2) the rise in the price of oil and the rapid accumulation of petrodollars in the oil countries and the Arab-U.S. rapprochement following the October War, 1974-75; (3) the rise of Saudi Arabia's significance, particularly with the eventual fall of the Shah, in 1978-79; and (4) the United States' response to the Soviet invasion of Afghanistan. These agreements are also supported by direct deployment of U.S. forces in the Indian Ocean or in Diego Garcia.

Sixth, because diplomatic relations have been severed between the United States and Iraq since 1967 and between the United States and Iran since 1979, the defense agreements concluded between Washington and each of these two countries have been excluded from this discussion. Also excluded in Qatar because, as of this writing, Qatar seems to be the only gulf state that has not concluded a defense agreement with the United States.

TABLE 5.1

Defense Agreements between the United States and Certain Gulf Countries (1981)

Country	Agreement	Date
Bahrain	Agreement relating to the status of personnel in the administrative support unit in Bahrain.	June 28, 1977
Iran	Memorandum concerning revisions of Foreign Military Sales' offers and acceptances between the United States and Iran (last agreement before the Shah left Iran).	October 19, 1979
	Hostages agreement.	January 19, 1981
Iraq	Military assistance.	December 3, 1955
	Terminated.	July 21, 1959
Kuwait	Agreement concerning the procurement of defense articles and defense services by Kuwait and the establishment of a U.S. liaison office in Kuwait.	April 15, 1975
Oman	Agreement to the provision of technical assistance and services to the Directorate General of Civil Aviation of Oman.	July 1, 1980
	Agreement concerning the use of certain facilities in Oman by the United States.	June 4, 1980
	Economic and technical cooperation agreement.	August 19, 1980
Saudi Arabia	Agreements relating to:	
	Transfer of military supplies and equipment.	June 18, 1951
	Military assistance advisory group.	June 27, 1953

Country	Agreement	Date
	Loan of F-86 aircraft to Saudi Arabia.	November 13, 1962
	Construction of certain military facilities in Saudi Arabia.	June 5, 1965
	Extended.	August 7, 1978
	Transfer of F-86 aircraft to Saudi Arabia.	November 11, 1965
	Privileges and immunities of U.S. personnel engaged in maintenance and operations of F-15 aircraft in Saudi Arabia.	July 5, 1972
	Deposit by Saudi Arabia of 10 percent of value of grant military assistance provided by the United States.	May 15, 1972
	Modernization program of the Saudi Arabian National Guard.	March 19, 1973
	Cooperation in the fields of economics, technology, industry, and defense.	June 8, 1974
	Technical cooperation.	May 12, 1975
	Extended.	May 25, 1979
	Related agreement.	September 5, 1980
	Manpower training and development.	August 6, 1976
	U.S. military training mission in Saudi Arabia.	February 27, 1977
United Arab Emirates	Agreement relating to the sale of defense articles and services.	June 21, 1975
United Kingdom	Agreement concerning a U.S. naval support facility on Diego Garcia, which is a British Indian Ocean territory.	February 25, 1976

Source: Treaties in Force: A List of Treaties and Other International Agreements of the United States in Force on January 1, 1981 (Washington, D.C.: U.S. Government Printing Office, 1981).

In addition to the above agreements, the United States has expanded its military assistance to Oman, Somalia, and Kenya, has improved its military facilities in both countries (including Oman's Masirah island) and on Diego Garcia. At least $140 million were committed to these projects in fiscal year 1981.[41] Under the United States-Omani foreign military sales agreements of mid-1980, Oman received from the United States during the 1980-82 period the following major military equipment: tanks, tank transporters, sidewinder air-to-air missiles, C130 transport aircraft, TOW antitank launchers and missiles, 155 mm. howitzers, trucks, tank ammunition, and tank-training teams.[42] Furthermore, under the 1981 military contract (MILCON) in Oman covering the Masirah Mobilization Camp, the United States was expected to upgrade the runway at Khasab (Musandam peninsula) and to send Corps of Engineers construction teams to start work on the Masirah Mobilization Camp project and other projects throughout Oman.[43]

In response to questions submitted by the Congressional Subcommittee on Europe and the Middle East, the Department of Defense highlighted several points concerning the importance of Oman and Somalia in enhancing U.S. military capabilities in the Persian Gulf. It should be pointed out, however, that specific answers to many of these questions were deleted from the public record for security reasons. It might be instructive to list some of the questions that were not answered for security reasons:

> What increased economic and military assistance have we agreed to provide to Somalia in exchange for access to Somalia's air and port facilities, especially at Berbera?
>
> What is the strategic advantage of United States access to facilities in Oman? How will this access enable us to project power into the Persian Gulf? Would United States ships homeport in Oman? What is the difference between what we will be doing in Oman and what we now do in Bahrain?
>
> What facilities in Oman, or Masirah Island and elsewhere, will the United States be improving and modifying to meet United States military needs?
>
> Is this new United States arrangement with Oman, in effect, a commitment to the security of Oman and a statement of intention to defend Oman against external attack?[44]

In response to questions about Diego Garcia and its role in U.S. power projection in the region, the Department of Defense made two specific points:

1. Diego Garcia is the single most important
facility for logistics and communications support of
the Naval Task Forces now deployed in the Arabian
Sea. It is also an important base for sea surveillance
flights. . . . The planned expansion of Diego Garcia
facilities will permit higher levels of support of the
Rapid Deployment Force.

2. The Naval Communications Station on Diego
Garcia is essential to Indian Ocean operations. . . .
The air facility has a great value as a base for ocean
surveillance, reconnaissance, and anti-submarine
patrols. [45]

In addition to the Omani facilities, the United States has dramatically raised the level of its participation in bolstering Saudi
Arabia's military capability through the sale of United States' AWACS
in October 1981. The AWACS were one element of the fourfold military sales package; the other three were air-refueling tankers, con-
formal fuel tanks for the F-15 planes already purchased by the
Saudis, and air-to-air missiles. This sale was designed to create
a high degree of long-term U.S.-Saudi cooperation in the military
and technical fields. It will also involve the presence of U.S. personnel in Saudi Arabia to maintain and support these weapons systems. [46]

The AWACS sale was seen by some critics as a part of a new
U.S. strategy for the Persian Gulf, particularly the oil fields of
Saudi Arabia, which would involve the building of "surrogate" bases
that would be used by U.S. forces in case of emergency. A Saudi
military infrastructure of this caliber would be used by U.S. air and
naval forces if the oil fields faced a serious threat. According to
this view, this "secret" U.S. strategy "would allow the United States
Rapid Deployment Force to move 'over the horizon' to these forward
bases and prepositioned supplies if the Soviet Union or other hostile
forces attempted to capture the Persian Gulf oil fields. . . ."[47]

In testifying in Congress on behalf of the AWACS sale on October 1, 1981, under secretary of state for security assistance,
science and technology, James L. Buckley, underscored the fact
that the AWACS were part of an ambitious strategy to protect the
gulf oil fields. This strategy would perform three essential and
interconnected functions: "help our friends cope with regional
threats, enhance the security of the West's principal sources of
imported oil, and establish an infrastructure that can receive and
support our Rapid Deployment Forces should we need to dispatch
them to meet a major challenge."[48] Under Secretary Buckley also
stated that Saudi Arabia was the centerpiece of this strategy and

that Saudi cooperation was crucial. According to Buckley, Saudi Arabia spearheads the pro-Western forces of moderation in the Muslim world and offers "a non-radical approach to modernization."[49]

The Rapid Deployment Joint Task Force (RDJTF) is the centerpiece of the United States' strategy to counter the perceived Soviet threat in the Persian Gulf/Arabian Peninsula. This entire Southwest Asia (SWA) area, the Soviet threat, and the RDJTF were discussed at length by Secretary of Defense Caspar W. Weinberger in his annual report to Congress on the 1983 budget. Secretary Weinberger stated that the events that have occurred in that region since 1979 "have dramatically increased the Soviet Union's access to the Persian Gulf region."[50] Secretary Weinberger envisioned the U.S. strategy for Southwest Asia in the 1980s to consist of two principal goals: "to improve our mobility forces and preposition adequate equipment and supplies to deploy and support an RDJTF of sufficient size to deter Soviet aggression; and to provide long-term support and resupply to sustain these forces."[51]

The rapid deployment strategy recognizes six special requirements:

> sustaining a continuous combat presence in a distant region halfway around the world;
> training our combat units for operations in unfamiliar and widely varying climates and terrain;
> tailoring support for unique and austere combat operations in a region lacking support facilities . . . and a highly developed infrastructure to provide them;
> developing mobility assets to deploy the RDJTF rapidly to and within SWA over extended air and sea lines of communication (ALOCs/SLOCs) and to sustain its operations in combat;
> obtaining from several other countries overflight rights and en route access; and
> securing lengthy ALOCs/SLOCs during the conflict to sustain combat operations.[52]

The Rapid Deployment Joint Task Force, which reports directly to the Department of Defense National Command Authority, has since October 1981 been set up as a separate force under a full-time commander with sole responsibility for Southwest Asia. The commander has been given control over several army units and air force tactical fighter squadrons. The RDJTF can draw on combat forces from the different services (see Table 5.2).

TABLE 5.2

Types of Combat Forces Available to the
Rapid Deployment Joint Task Force

Number	Combat Force
Army	
1	Airborne division
1	Air mobile/air assault division
1	Cavalry brigade air combat (CBAC)
1	Mechanized infantry division
Rangers and unconventional warfare units	
Marines	
1-2	Marine amphibious forces (MAF)*
Air Force	
4-11	Air Force tactical fighter wings (with support air forces)
2	Squadrons of strategic bombers (the Strategic Projection Force)
Navy	
3	Carrier battle groups (CVBGs)
1	Surface action group
5	Air-ASW patrol squadrons (VP)
Headquarters	
1	Army corps headquarters
1	Naval forces headquarters
1	Air Force forces headquarters

*An MAF typically consists of a reinforced Marine division and a Marine aircraft wing (roughly twice the size of an Air Force tactical fighter wing).

Source: Caspar W. Weinberger, Annual Report to the Congress (Washington, D.C.: U.S. Government Printing Office, February 8, 1982), p. III-103.

COMMAND MIDDLE EAST FORCE

One of the oldest defense agreements between the United States and a gulf country has dealt with the presence of Washington's Middle East Force (MIDEASTFOR) in the Persian Gulf, with homeporting facilities in Bahrain. MIDEASTFOR first entered the gulf in 1949 as the result of an agreement with Britain, which at the time exercised a protectorate status over Bahrain. After Bahrain became independent in 1971, the agreement covering MIDEASTFOR was concluded directly with Bahrain.

This agreement is interesting for several reasons; the most important is that it is a microcosm of the difficulties, misperceptions, confused definitions of security, and local nationalistic feelings that usually accompany any overt foreign military presence in a politically sensitive area. This agreement, also known as the Jufair agreement, has frequently been the focus of controversy both within Bahrain and between Bahrain and some of its neighbors. More recently, it has been at the center of the dichotomy resulting from the gulf states' need for U.S. military protection versus their dislike for U.S. military presence. Secondly, it would be wise for Washington's policy makers to study the background of the Jufair agreement, because of its acceptance by the government but its frequent rejection by the people. The Jufair agreement has often been perceived by political elites in Bahrain and elsewhere in the gulf as supporting family rule and as a pretext for the establishment of a foreign military foothold in the region. This view is not necessarily shared by a majority of the country's elites and certainly not by the business elites. The MIDEASTFOR agreement offers a useful case study of the sensitive nature of basing and facilities arrangements in that volatile region.

To place MIDEASTFOR in proper perspective, it is a very small naval force that for years has consisted of a flagship and two small destroyers. Since late 1979, the force has been increased to five ships. MIDEASTFOR is commanded by a rear admiral, whose primary function has been to pay friendly visits to countries in the area to show the flag. As a low-key symbol of U.S. interest, the three COMIDEASTFOR ships served during the 1950s and 1960s on a rotational basis until the flagship began to homeport in Bahrain in 1966. [53]

Following the British announcement regarding their withdrawal from "East of Suez" by 1971, and in view of increased Soviet naval activity in the Indian Ocean, the United States decided to keep COMIDEASTFOR in the gulf. The agreement to deploy COMIDEAST-FOR in Bahrain was concluded by exchange of notes in Manama, Bahrain, on December 23, 1971 by the U.S. chargé d'affaires and by the foreign minister of Bahrain. The agreement indicated on-shore facilities available to naval personnel and their juridical status as U.S. citizens.

The deployment agreement was deposited with the United Nations and was published in official treaty sources of the U.S. government. [54] It was also discussed in the Senate and of course the U.S. press. However, in Bahrain itself the agreement has not been published by the government, and it has not been discussed in any detail in the local press. In early 1975, the National Assembly questioned the government concerning the deployment agreement, and the government immediately requested that the agreement be discussed in an executive session. [55]

The Jufair agreement was signed on December 23, 1971, but the State Department did not disclose the accord until January 5, 1972. At least two factors were involved in this delay: Bahrain's sensitivity to a U.S. presence on the island and the desire of the Nixon administration to deemphasize the agreement, hoping that a low profile would avoid a confrontation with the Senate over the use of executive agreements. The administration maintained that the agreement contained "no defense or political commitment whatsoever"; it was simply a continuation of the arrangements concerning the Jufair facilities that the Navy had made with Britain prior to Bahrain's independence. [56] Rear Admiral M. G. Bayne, the first commander of MIDEASTFOR in Bahrain under the new agreement, publicly stated that the primary mission of the U.S. Navy in Bahrain would be to carry out goodwill visits to the countries of the region and that the activities of the U.S. Navy in the gulf would involve the establishment and maintenance of harmonious and cooperative relations among the governments and peoples of the region. [57] Rear Admiral Robert Hanks, who replaced Admiral Bayne, expressed similar views. [58]

However, the announcement of the agreement in January 1972 aroused the members of the Senate Foreign Relations Committee. Senator Clifford Case (Rep.—N.J.) responded to the government's disclosure of the navy's stationing agreements with Bahrain and Portugal by stating that "the establishment of an American base in a foreign country is a very serious matter, which should require the advice and consent of the Senate." [59] On March 3, 1972, the Senate adopted Resolution 214 by a 50-6 vote to the effect that "any agreement with Portugal or Bahrain for military bases or foreign assistance should be submitted as a treaty to the Senate for advice and consent." [60] The administration intensified its lobbying among the senators to extricate Bahrain from the resolution, arguing that a formal treaty would embarrass Bahrain with its Arab neighbors. Senator Hugh Scott (Rep.—Pa.) led the lobbying efforts of the administration, pointing out that the deployment agreement was a sensitive matter, that the disclosure was delayed at the request of the Bahraini government, and that if the Senate "persisted in requiring a treaty, he suspected that Bahrain might cancel the arrangement."[61]

On May 23, 1972, the Senate Foreign Relations Committee approved a bill as an amendment to Resolution 214, which barred funds for the implementation of the naval base agreement with Bahrain until the agreement should be submitted to the Senate for approval. On June 28, 1972, however, the Senate voted down this amendment (59-30). The agreement was in fact enforced without major incident until October 20, 1973.

On that day, the Bahraini government served a notice to the U.S. government to terminate the lease in one year, on October 20, 1974. However, emotions had calmed down by the following October and the Bahraini government did not force the issue. Bargaining and negotiations over the amount of rent that the Bahrainis wanted the United States to pay for the facilities at Jufair continued for some time. The 1971 agreement was renegotiated in 1975; however, the renegotiated Status of Forces Agreement (SOFA) dealt primarily with Bahraini sovereign jurisdiction over offenses committed by U.S. Navy personnel in Bahrain.[62]

The agreement in its entirety was renegotiated in 1977, resulting in a new kind of agreement. Whereas the earlier agreement used the phrase "United States Force," the 1977 agreement used "Administrative Support Unit."[63] This change was essentially a public relations effort by the Bahraini government to mollify its critics. The term "personnel of the Administrative Support Unit" is defined in Article 12 of the 1977 agreement to mean:

> U.S. Department of Defense personnel who may reside in or visit Bahrain after June 30, 1977, for purposes related to the functions of the Administrative Support Unit, including dependents, and including personnel aboard ships and aircraft visiting Bahrain supported by the Administrative Support Unit, but excluding indigenous Bahraini nationals and other persons ordinarily resident in Bahrain territory, provided that such nationals or other persons are not dependents of members of the Administrative Support Unit.[64]

Following the signing of the first Jufair agreement in 1971, Bahrain's foreign minister, Shaikh Muhammad bin Mubarak al-Khalifa, defended the agreement, which some Arabs criticized, by saying that the agreement was simply a commercial arrangement. The government's official and diplomatic perception of the agreement has been based on four assumptions: the agreement was solely commercial; Bahrain's sovereignty and independence were not being infringed upon by the agreement; the agreement did not demand any military or political commitments by either signatory; and the agreement would benefit the national economy. [65]

Psychological security has been another factor in the government's perception of the Jufair agreement. The British withdrawal left Persian Gulf rulers, shaikhs, and amirs very concerned for their future survival. They viewed the incipient radicalism in the gulf with apprehension. The presence of a visible Western military force, no matter how small, would be a symbol of security to the rulers and an indirect warning to radical movements against any serious tampering with the status quo. The al-Khalifas of Bahrain perceived the Jufair agreement as precisely this symbol of security. [66]

However, the regional situation has changed dramatically since the early 1970s, and even more so since the summer of 1977, when the "Administrative Support Unit" agreement was signed. COMIDEASTFOR is still on location, and its task has become much more strategically oriented than showing the flag on friendly visits. However, it has been overshadowed by the formation, deployment, and even politics of the Rapid Deployment Joint Task Force.

One can clearly conclude that since 1981 the United States has embarked on an ambitious and complex strategy to protect the security of Southwest Asia. This region encompasses the Persian Gulf, the Arabian Peninsula, the Gulf of Oman, the Red Sea, the northwest corner of the Indian Ocean, and the Horn of Africa. The primary local countries that have joined this security arrangement are Saudi Arabia, Oman, Somalia, and Kenya. Britain's involvement is through Diego Garcia. The Southwest Asia strategy will involve billions of dollars during the 1980s and will require the continuous cooperation of the local states, particularly Saudi Arabia. How dependable is this cooperation? What if Saudi Arabia, because of possible political disagreements with the United States, decides to terminate its participation in this strategy? Will the United States force the Saudis to participate? The next chapter of this book will offer some reflections on these and other questions.

NOTES

1. Walter Millis, ed., The Forrestal Diaries (New York: Viking Press, 1951), p. 272.

2. Ibid., p. 323.

3. Ibid., p. 358.

4. Ibid., p. 359.

5. Ibid., p. 324.

6. Ibid., p. 359.

7. Dwight D. Eisenhower, Mandate for Change, 1953-1956 (New York: Doubleday, 1963), pp. 159-66.

8. Theodore C. Sorensen, Kennedy (New York: Harper & Row, 1965), p. 628.

9. Arthur M. Schlesinger, Jr., A Thousand Days: John F. Kennedy in the White House (Boston: Houghton Mifflin, 1965), pp. 566-67.

10. Public Papers of the Presidents of the United States, Lyndon B. Johnson, 1967, I (Washington, D.C.: U.S. Government Printing Office, 1968), pp. 633-34.

11. Public Papers of the Presidents of the United States, Lyndon B. Johnson, 1967, II (Washington, D.C.: U.S. Government Printing Office, 1968), pp. 801-2.

12. Public Papers of the Presidents of the United States, Richard Nixon, 1969 (Washington, D.C.: U.S. Government Printing Office, 1971), pp. 68-69.

13. Public Papers of the Presidents of the United States, Richard Nixon, 1970 (Washington, D.C.: U.S. Government Printing Office, 1971), p. 558.

14. Ibid.

15. Public Papers of the Presidents of the United States, Richard Nixon, 1972 (Washington, D.C.: U.S. Government Printing Office, 1974), p. 291.

16. Ibid., p. 290.

17. Public Papers of the Presidents of the United States, Richard Nixon, 1973 (Washington, D.C.: U.S. Government Printing Office, 1975), p. 452.

18. Ibid., p. 451.

19. U.S. Interests in the Policy Toward the Persian Gulf. Hearings before the Subcommittee on the Near East of the Committee on Foreign Affairs, House of Representatives, 92nd Cong., 2nd sess. (Washington, D.C.: U.S. Government Printing Office, 1972), p. 82.

20. Ibid.

21. Ibid.

22. Ibid.

23. Ibid., pp. 82-83.

24. Ibid., p. 83.

25. Ibid.

26. Ibid., p. 85.

27. Public Papers of the Presidents of the United States, Richard Nixon, 1973, pp. 871, 902, 916-17, 938-41; Richard Nixon,

1974, pp. 473-74, 506-10; Gerald R. Ford, 1974 (Washington, D.C.: U.S. Government Printing Office, 1975), pp. 12, 61, 680, 684; Gerald R. Ford, 1975, I (Washington, D.C.: U.S. Government Printing Office, 1977), pp. 63, 65-66, 97-100, 289, 552-54, 674-75, 717-19; Gerald R. Ford, 1975, II (Washington, D.C.: U.S. Government Printing Office, 1977), pp. 1238-39, 1505, 1766-67; Jimmy Carter, 1977, I (Washington, D.C.: U.S. Government Printing Office, 1978), pp. 386-87, 600-1, 768-69, 861-62, 947, 991-93, 1006-8, 1010-12; Jimmy Carter, 1977, II (Washington, D.C.: U.S. Government Printing Office, 1978), pp. 1515-16, 1720-22, 1747-48, 1896-98, 1954-57, 2029-32, 2188-91, 2217-18, 2220-22; Weekly Compilation of Presidential Documents vol. 14 (1978), pp. 1590, 1770-80, 1876-77, 2018-20, 2101, 2172-73, 2226, 2255-56; ibid., vol. 15 (1979), pp. 50-52, 101, 157, 159, 245, 301-4, 310-16, 349-52, 453-59, 565, 610-11, 685.

28. Department of State Bulletin 69 (July 2, 1973):30-31; New Perspectives on the Persian Gulf. Hearings before the Subcommittee on the Near East and South Asia of the Committee on Foreign Affairs, House of Representatives, 93rd Cong., 1st sess. (Washington, D.C.: U.S. Government Printing Office, 1973), p. 2.

29. The Persian Gulf, 1974: Money, Politics, Arms and Power. Hearings before the Subcommittee on Foreign Affairs, House of Representatives, 93rd Cong., 2nd sess. (Washington, D.C.: U.S. Government Printing Office, 1975), p. 73.

30. Ibid., pp. 61-62.

31. The Persian Gulf, 1975: The Continuing Debate on Arms Sales. Hearings before the Special Subcommittee on Investigations of the Committee on International Relations, House of Representatives, 94th Cong., 1st sess. (Washington, D.C.: U.S. Government Printing Office, 1976), p. 9.

32. Ibid., p. 12.

33. Department of State Bulletin 80 (May 1980):63.

34. U.S. Interests in, and Policies Toward, the Persian Gulf, 1980. Hearings before the Subcommittee on Europe and the Middle East of the Committee on Foreign Affairs, House of Representatives, 96th Cong., 2nd sess. (Washington, D.C.: U.S. Government Printing Office, 1980), p. 338.

35. Ibid.

36. Ibid.

37. U.S. Strategy in the Middle East. Current Policy no. 312 (Washington, D.C.: Department of State, Bureau of Public Affairs, September 17, 1981), p. 1.

38. Ibid., p. 2.

39. Saudi Security, Middle East Peace, and U.S. Interests. Current Policy no. 323 (Washington, D.C.: Department of State, Bureau of Public Affairs, October 1, 1981), p. 2.

40. Treaties in Force: A List of Treaties and Other International Agreements of the United States in Force on January 1, 1981 (Washington, D.C.: U.S. Government Printing Office, 1981), pp. 11, 101-4, 126, 160, 186-87, 219.

41. U.S. Interests in, and Policies Toward, the Persian Gulf, 1980, p. 93.

42. Foreign Assistance Legislation for Fiscal Year 1982 (pt. 3). Hearings and Markup before the Subcommittee on Europe and the Middle East of the Committee on Foreign Affairs, House of Representatives, 97th Cong., 1st sess. (Washington, D.C.: U.S. Government Printing Office, 1981), p. 82.

43. Ibid., p. 84.

44. U.S. Interests in, and Policies Toward, the Persian Gulf, 1980, p. 413.

45. Ibid., pp. 413-14.

46. Proposed Sale of Airborne Warning and Control Systems (AWACS) and F-15 Enhancements to Saudi Arabia. Hearings and Markup before the Committee on Foreign Affairs and Its Subcommittees on International Security and Scientific Affairs and on Europe and the Middle East, House of Representatives, 97th Cong., 1st sess. (Washington, D.C.: U.S. Government Printing Office, 1981), p. 40.

47. Scott Armstrong, "Saudis' AWACS Just a Beginning of New Strategy," Washington Post, November 1, 1981, p. A1.

48. Airborne Warning and Control Systems, p. 39.

49. Ibid.

50. Caspar W. Weinberger, Annual Report to the Congress. Report on the FY 1983 budget, FY 1984 authorization request, and FY 1983-87 defense programs (Washington, D.C.: U.S. Government Printing Office, February 8, 1982), p. II-19.

51. Ibid., pp. III-104-5.

52. Ibid., p. III-104.

53. Peter W. DeForth, "U.S. Naval Presence in the Persian Gulf: The Mideast Force Since World War II," Naval War College Review 28 (Summer 1975):28-38.

54. United States Treaties and Other International Agreements, vol. 22, pt. 2 (1971), pp. 2184-89.

55. State of Bahrain, Official Gazette Supplement: Record of the National Assembly, 19th sess., January 26, 1975, p. 8.

56. Department of State Bulletin, February 8, 1972, p. 282.

57. Personal interview, October 28, 1972.

58. Personal interview, January 27, 1973.

59. New York Times, January 7, 1972.

60. U.S., Congress, Senate, Committee on Foreign Relations and House of Representatives, Committee on International

Relations, Legislation on Foreign Relations with Explanatory Notes
(Washington, D.C.: U.S. Government Printing Office, June 1975),
p. 1073.

61. Washington Post, July 1, 1972.

62. United States Treaties and Other International Agreements, vol. 26, pt. 3 (1975), pp. 3027-30.

63. Ibid., vol. 28, pt. 5 (1977), pp. 5312-16.

64. Ibid., p. 5314.

65. Sada al-'Usbu' (Bahrain), January 11, 1972.

66. Personal interviews with Bahraini officials in 1972-73.

6

PROBLEMS AND PROSPECTS: TOWARD PARTNERSHIP

OVERVIEW

The triangular relationship involving the United States, the Persian Gulf, and the Palestinian conflict is persistent, complex, and not subject to easy solutions. It is also fraught with complications over which the parties involved have little or no control. The U.S. involvement in the gulf is increasing in magnitude, and Washington's pursuit of its interests, particularly since early 1980, has become more visible, as have the policies of the gulf states. Both the United States and the gulf states have openly identified their objectives and embarked on specific courses of action to achieve them.

The United States, for example, has identified two primary objectives: "assuring access to oil and keeping the Soviets out of the region."[1] In the process, the United States has adopted specific policies, such as the establishment of the Rapid Deployment Joint Task Force, to reflect U.S. readiness to deal with any threat that might seriously interfere with these two objectives. The gulf Arab states have also identified certain political and economic objectives and have initiated policies to realize these objectives. Among these objectives are protecting the security of the region, maintaining internal stability, and nurturing economic cooperation. These objectives apply more properly to the family-ruled states, including Saudi Arabia. While Iraq has supported these objectives, it has been preoccupied with the conflict with Iran. Iran has also been preoccupied both with internal matters and with its war with Iraq. Furthermore, since the United States has no diplomatic relations with either Iran or Iraq, its policies have perforce focused on the other states. Accordingly, the discussion of U.S.-Persian Gulf partnership has so far focused on relations with Saudi Arabia, Oman, Kuwait, Bahrain, Qatar, and the United Arab Emirates, with Saudi Arabia and Oman comprising the largest share of the U.S. connection.

Political, economic, and military policies in the gulf have been, and will continue to be, subject to constraints and dangers that emanate both from within and outside the region. On the military front, the difficulties facing United States' efforts are "the distance from the United States; the lack of bases; [and] the proximity to the Soviet Union."[2] In view of these difficulties, the credibility of any U.S. military action or threat of action would be hard to evaluate. Such predictability is related to at least four factors: "the degree of Soviet involvement, the interest and willingness of our West European and Asian allies to be involved, the legitimacy of government of the country to be protected, and the availability of bases and facilities."[3]

Addressing a gathering at the Johns Hopkins School of Advanced International Studies in April 1981, former Secretary of Defense Harold Brown delineated some of the dangers and real difficulties facing the United States in its attempt to build a security framework in the Persian Gulf. The potential dangers involve one or all of the following: internal conflict within the oil-producing states; a cutoff of a major portion of the supply of oil; an expanding Soviet political and ideological dominance in some influential groups; and a direct Soviet military conquest of the oil fields.[4]

The building of a security framework will also be hindered by several difficulties, including the religious, ethnic, and tribal divisions within the political structure of Muslim gulf countries, the continued Arab-Israeli conflict, the socioeconomic tensions that accompany the simultaneous existence of abject poverty and abundant wealth in the region, and the lack of developed political structures in many of these countries.[5] Although the Arab-Israeli conflict is not the only conflict in the region, according to Secretary Brown, it "has an intensifying effect" on the other conflicts.[6] The United States should therefore expand its efforts to effect a settlement of the conflict, "including the prospect of some settlement of the Palestinian issue."[7] He also called on the United States and its industrialized allies to set up a comprehensive program of "economic development assistance to those more populous and militarily important nations of the region that do not have economic resources that go with oil production."[8]

These same two themes were cited a year later by an Omani official in a newspaper interview. Responding to a question about the future of United States-Omani political relations and the limits of cooperation between the United States and Oman, the Omani minister of state for foreign affairs, Youssef Alawi, indicated that a resolution of the Palestinian conflict and a comprehensive economic and military aid program are prerequisites for closer U.S. relations with Oman and other gulf states. [9]

OIL ISSUES

The industrial countries' dependence on Persian Gulf oil is continuing, and therefore the United States and its allies cannot be oblivious to regional developments that will affect, positively or negatively, continued access to gulf oil. This concern must be rational, realistic, and nonbelligerent. After all, the "energy crisis" was caused by excessive consumption and the lack of an energy policy in the industrial nations. It was not as if a "Persian Gulf fleet appeared in New York Harbor demanding that we open the United States to foreign trade."[10] The energy crisis, as far as the United States is concerned, has been perpetuated by two factors: the lack of a national energy policy and the dependence on, and unpredictability of, imported oil.

Presidential task forces on energy since the 1950s have equated imported oil with national security and have generally recommended that restrictions be placed on oil imports. In a 1970 report on oil and national security, the cabinet task force noted that many risks are potentially involved in this dependence on foreign oil. These include the possibility of a prolonged war, terrorist threats to oil tankers on the high seas, local revolutions, the ascendancy to power of radical governments in major oil-producing countries, the banding together of oil producers in a strong cartel, an oil embargo against some or all Western oil consumers, and the possibility that the oil countries might nationalize their oil companies. [11]

In another report on energy, further research was recommended regarding the future availability of oil. Such research would provide answers to basic questions dealing with the oil producers' "enduring capacity to cooperate in a strong cartel," with their ability to control the marketing and pricing of oil on international markets, and with the ability of the consuming countries to prevent the oil prices from rising.[12] According to the report, what tended to exacerbate the situation was the fact that the oil trade is dominated by large international companies, a majority of which are U.S. corporations, and that international oil and international politics could not be kept separate.[13]

A brief look at the energy question in the late 1960s and early 1970s indicates that, within the span of a very few years, oil consumption, oil scarcity, and oil prices took what seemed to be a sudden upward jump. Although the search for alternative energy sources intensified, no real energy substitute was developed, and one is not expected before the turn of the century. Furthermore, in the late 1960s and early 1970s, the oil companies began to lose their grip on the production of oil; OPEC became influential, the oil countries became richer and more politicized, and, of course, the oil weapon was unleashed.[14]

By far the most ambitious energy project devised by the U.S. government was President Nixon's 1974 Project Independence.[15] The project initiated the most comprehensive energy research and analysis ever taken. The ultimate goal was to make the United States independent of foreign energy sources by 1980. In introducing the Project Independence Report, Federal Energy Administrator John C. Sawhill said that the purpose of this undertaking was "to evaluate the nation's energy problems and provide a framework for developing a national energy policy."[16] The report's attempt to develop a comprehensive national energy policy was guided by the examination of four different strategies:

To increase production from domestic sources;
To reduce or restructure domestic energy demand;
To establish domestic programs or policies to reduce adverse consequences of a disruption in energy supplies or prices (contingency plans, storage, fuel switching, etc.); and
To take steps in the international area to reduce the likelihood of a disruption of imports.[17]

The basic premise of Project Independence was "that while imported oil is potentially cheap, it may also be unreliable."[18] Through a program of national energy independence, the project framers envisioned that it would be feasible to reduce oil imports "to the lowest level deemed economically and socially acceptable."[19]

The project was conceived in March 1974, and the Project Independence Report was completed in November of the same year. By the time the report was completed, it became painfully apparent to many U.S. officials that the price of oil was already making its projections dated. For example, between late 1973 and late 1974, the price of oil quadrupled, rising from roughly $2.50 a barrel to about $10.00 a barrel. The figures used in the report for purposes of oil projections to 1985 were $4, $7, and $11 respectively. By the end of the 1970s, the price of a barrel of oil had already topped $30.00. U.S. dependence on gulf oil was more pronounced than ever; over 50 percent of the total oil consumption in the industrial countries of the world was imported. Petrodollars accumulated at unprecedented levels both in the producing countries and in Western banking and financial institutions. By 1980, Project Independence had all but faded into the archives of contemporary U.S. history.

The 1980s began with the Persian Gulf occupying an unquestioned preeminence in U.S. foreign policy planning because of its oil resources. In terms of oil production, estimated crude oil reserves, and exports to the industrial world, gulf oil will continue to be sought after until at least the year 2000. Table 6.1 illustrates the significance of the OPEC countries as a source of oil. Except for Bahrain and Oman, the major gulf oil countries are all members of OPEC. Of the total world crude oil reserves (568.6 billion barrels) as of January 1, 1979, OPEC had 382.6 billion barrels or 67.3 percent; the United States had 27.8 billion barrels or 4.9 percent. The eight gulf countries (Iran, Iraq, Saudi Arabia, Kuwait, Qatar, Bahrain, United Arab Emirates, and Oman) accounted for 52.7 percent, with Saudi Arabia holding the largest individual share (19.9 percent). Table 6.2 gives a breakdown of similar data.

The United States, Western Europe, and Japan continue to import crude oil from the gulf. The U.S. imports of gulf oil and the cost of this oil are staggering. To illustrate, in 1970 the U.S. oil import bill was $2.7 billion; in 1980 it reached $90 billion. During this ten-year period, the oil import bill made two dramatic jumps: in the 1973-74 period, from $7.7 billion to $26.3 billion and in the 1979-80 period, from $56.5 billion to $90 billion (see Table 6.3).

The significance of the Persian Gulf as a source of oil for the industrial world cannot be overemphasized when one analyzes the oil imports of the consuming countries. According to the 1979 estimates, 31 percent of the total amount of the United States' imported oil came from the Persian Gulf, 73 percent of Japan's imports, and 63 percent of Western Europe's imports, as shown in Table 6.4. In Western Europe, West Germany, France, and Italy are the largest importers of oil and also of gulf oil.[20] The picture is not expected to change appreciably by 1985. Therefore, U.S. relations with the Persian Gulf will be largely governed by the need for oil for at least the remainder of the century. Cognizant of this fact, it is no wonder that continued accessibility to gulf oil has become a cardinal principle of U.S. foreign policy, a principle that the United States has indicated that it would spare no effort to defend.

ARMS POLICIES

To guarantee accessibility to gulf oil and to protect gulf security, the United States has embarked on a comprehensive policy of arms sales to local states. However, this policy of stability through the sale of U.S. arms has labored under many constraints, some of

TABLE 6.1

World Oil Supply and Demand
(million barrels per day)

Region	1979 Supply	1979 Demand	1990 Supply	1990 Demand	2000 Supply	2000 Demand
U.S. and Canada	12	(U.S.) 18 NA*	9	(U.S.) 16 NA	9	(U.S.) 15 NA
Western Europe	2	15	4	13	4	13
Other non-OPEC	6	NA	10	NA	13	NA
OPEC	32	NA	30	NA	29	NA
Centrally planned economies	14	13	15	15	16	16
Japan	NA	5	NA	5	NA	5
Other industrial countries	NA	4	NA	4	NA	4
Developing countries	NA	11	NA	17	NA	24

*NA is either not available or negligible.
Source: Exxon Corporation, World Energy Outlook (December 1980), pp. 21-22.

TABLE 6.2

Estimates of Petroleum Reserves in Selected Countries
and Crude Oil Production in 1978
(in thousands of barrels)

Country	Estimated Reserves at January 1, 1979	Percent World Reserves at January 1, 1979	Crude Oil Production 1978
Bahrain	269,482	0.05	19,345
Iran[a]	44,965,650	7.91	1,900,555
Iraq[a]	34,392,020	6.06	959,585
Kuwait	71,400,000	12.56	680,725
Neutral zone[b]	6,171,500	1.10	170,090
Oman	3,271,404	0.58	115,300
Qatar	3,765,340	0.67	176,537
Saudi Arabia	113,284,000	19.92	3,113,470
United Arab Emirates	31,583,651	5.55	668,680
United States	27,803,760	4.89	3,175,927
Soviet Union	58,438,000	10.28	4,093,475

[a]Production dropped significantly during the border war.
[b]Borders on Iraq and Saudi Arabia.

Source: Twentieth Century Petroleum Statistics, 1979 (Dallas: DeGolyer and MacNaughton, 1979), p. 1.

TABLE 6.3

OPEC Oil Prices and Total U.S. Oil Import Bill
(1970–80)

Year	Benchmark Price/Barrel[a] (in dollars)	U.S. Oil Import Bill (in billions of dollars)
1970	1.80	2.74
1971	2.18	3.35
1972	2.48	4.36
1973	2.59	7.74
1974	10.95	26.26
1975	10.46	25.06
1976	11.51	32.11
1977	12.09	42.01
1978	12.70	39.60
1979[b]	13.34, 14.54, 24.00	56.51
1980[c]	26.00, 28.00	90.00

[a]Prices are normally set by the Saudi "benchmark" or "marker" light oil, which is more easily refined. However, actual prices have varied widely.

[b]Prices went up three times during the year.

[c]Two-tier pricing system in 1980.

Sources: U.S. Interests in, and Policies Toward, the Persian Gulf. Hearings before the Subcommittee on Europe and the Middle East of the Committee on Foreign Affairs, House of Representatives, 96th Cong., 2nd sess. (Washington, D.C.: U.S. Government Printing Office, 1980), p. 213; Washington Post, October 30, 1981, p. A25.

TABLE 6.4

Dependence on Persian Gulf Oil:
Estimates and Projections
(1979 and 1985)

	United States		Japan		Western Europe		Total	
	1979	1985	1979	1985	1979	1985	1979	1985
Oil imports (mbd)*	7.8	8	5.6	6	12.8	13.0	26.2	27.0
Imports from Persian Gulf (mbd)*	2.4	3	4.1	5	8.0	8.0	14.5	16.0
Percent of gulf imports to total imports	31	34	73	73	63	62	55	56

*Million barrels per day.

Source: U.S. Interests in, and Policies Toward, the Persian Gulf. Hearings before the Subcommittee on Europe and the Middle East of the Committee on Foreign Affairs, House of Representatives, 96th Cong., 2nd sess. (Washington, D.C.: U.S. Government Printing Office, 1980), p. 218.

which are caused by geography, others by ideology. The geographic constraints reflect two realities: the great distance separating the United States from the gulf, which raises doubts about the United States' logistical ability to fight an effective conventional war in the Persian Gulf region; and secondly, the physical and human topography of the local countries, that is, small populations, the lack of trained military personnel, and the small areas in which the oil fields are located. Legitimate questions can be raised regarding these countries' ability to participate in a sustained military operation, either in conjunction with other allies or in ability to fend off any aggressor until an allied force arrives.

Ideologically, the constraints focus on whether the local states feel comfortable about openly identifying with the U.S. military efforts, and by implication military presence, in the region. Yet, it is clear that if the United States were to successfully respond to a serious threat to the oil fields, it would need some bases or facilities in the countries for the positioning of forces and warehousing of supplies. This prompted the United States to conclude a facilities agreement with Oman in mid-1980. This agreement calls ultimately for the expenditure of several billion dollars for new and improved airfields, landing facilities, and other needed services. Indeed, the United States has in recent years provided Oman and other countries with all kinds of military supplies under both the Foreign Military Sales and the Arms Sales programs. [21]

The United States' military agreements with Saudi Arabia delineate the magnitude of these agreements and the importance that Washington attaches to gulf security and to Saudi Arabia's role in preserving this security. These agreements might also encourage public debate on the nature of the policy, which seems to rely so heavily on arms sales and military development with scant attention given to political questions. Tables 6.5 and 6.6 summarize the Foreign Military Sales agreements with Saudi Arabia and the major in-country projects involving the United States Army Corps of Engineers. Between 1975 and 1980, the United States–Saudi foreign sales agreements totaled over $30 billion, while the Army Corps of Engineers' agreements amounted to approximately $24 billion.

The principal defense modernization programs in Saudi Arabia in which the United States is involved include:

1. Extensive construction projects coordinated by the U.S. Army Corps of Engineers (military cantonments, schools, hospitals, airports, housing, and deepwater ports).

2. The Saudi Arabian Ordnance Corps Program (SOCP). The U.S. Defense Department undertook a long-range project to establish an integrated logistics system for the Saudi Ordnance Corps.

TABLE 6.5

United States–Saudi Arabian Foreign Military
Sales Agreements and Deliveries
(in thousands of dollars)

Fiscal Year	Agreements	Deliveries
1974	2,031,250	329,971
1975	3,614,819	324,239
1976	7,742,089	926,882
1977	1,888,155	1,502,104
1978	4,121,519	2,368,921
1979	6,468,701	2,471,531
1980	4,536,777	2,724,746
Total	30,403,310	10,648,394

Note: Agreements and deliveries include the value of Saudi
Arabian Engineer Assistance Agreements projects requested by
the Saudi Arabia minister of defense and aviation and approved by
the U.S. government for management by the U.S. Corps of Engineers.

Source: Saudi Arabia and the United States: The New Context in an Evolving "Special Relationship." Report prepared for
the Subcommittee on Europe and the Middle East of the Committee
on Foreign Affairs, House of Representatives by the Congressional
Research Service of the Library of Congress (Washington, D.C.:
U.S. Government Printing Office, 1981), p. 48.

TABLE 6.6

U.S. Army Corps of Engineers:
Saudi Arabian Program Review
(in millions of dollars)

Program	Department of Defense[a]	Cost Estimate
Status of program:		
Construction completed	1,546	1,488
Under construction	4,072	3,920
Out for contract bids	1,499	1,495
Under design	4,668	11,514
In planning	949	3,880
Total programs[b]	12,734	22,297
Components of program:		
Engineer assistance agreement[c]	8,510	14,140
Saudi Naval Expansion Program (SNEP)	2,455	4,688
Saudi Arabian National Guard (SANG)	369	2,010
Saudi Ordnance Corps Program (SOCP)	1,229	1,229
Ministry of Information	14	14
Other programs	1,387	1,445
Total programs	13,964	23,526

[a]Congress has approved cases totaling $25,000,000 or more.
[b]Excludes Saudi Ordnance Corps Program.
[c]Includes Air Force and Army construction activities.
Source: Saudi Arabia and the United States: The New Context in an Evolving "Special Relationship." Report prepared for the Subcommittee on Europe and the Middle East of the Committee on Foreign Affairs, House of Representatives by the Congressional Research Service of the Library of Congress (Washington, D.C.: U.S. Government Printing Office, 1981), p. 49.

3. The Saudi Naval Expansion Program (SNEP), which would modernize and expand the Saudi Royal Navy over a ten-year period.

4. The Royal Saudi Air Force Peace Hawk Program, which includes training, construction of support facilities, and acquisition of F-5 intercept/close-support aircraft.

5. The Royal Saudi Air Force Peace Sun Program, which includes training, construction of support facilities, and acquisition of 62 F-15 Eagle air superiority fighter aircraft.

6. The Saudi Arabian National Guard Modernization Program (SANG), which includes the modernization of SANG in such areas as organization, training, equipment procurement, supply, communication, and facilities.

7. The Royal Saudi Army Modernization Program, which includes the modernization of two infantry brigades by converting them to mechanized brigades and the sale of tanks, armored personnel carriers, howitzers, Redeye missile systems, Dragon missile systems, and air defense artillery.

8. The Hawk Air Defense System, which includes upgrading and improving the Saudi Hawk missile system in order to protect population centers at Jiddah, Riyadh, and Dhahran, defense sites such as Khamis Mushayt, al-Batin, and Tabuq, and the approaches to the oil-producing eastern province. [22]

This list of projects, which is by no means exhaustive, gives a synoptic picture of the intensity of Washington's involvement in the modernization of the Saudi defense capability. A similar type of involvement is in progress in the civilian sector of the Saudi socioeconomic infrastructure, in the context of the United States-Saudi Joint Commission on Economic Cooperation. [23]

It is important to realize that gulf countries are small and possess a limited military capability. Not only are they and their oil fields vulnerable, but it is doubtful whether any country can effectively defend itself against a sizable threat. Because of the small size of their defense forces, gulf countries would be easily overwhelmed by a major aggression from the outside (see Table 6.7). Although in recent years they have been modernizing their military capabilities at a frantic pace, their major weapons systems, particularly combat aircraft and tanks, are still relatively limited (see Table 6.8). Furthermore, it will be several years before these countries have enough trained indigenous personnel to operate the newly acquired or recently ordered sophisticated weapons systems at optimum efficiency. This means that United States' and West European military advisors will be involved in those countries at least through this decade. Of course, the basic question is: What would be the fate of these agreements and arms purchase orders in the event of political upheavals or changes of regime?

TABLE 6.7

Military Manpower in Persian Gulf States
(1981–82)

Country	Army	Navy	Air Force	Total
Bahrain	2,300	200	—	2,500
Iran	150,000	10,000	35,000	195,000[a]
Iraq	210,000	4,250	38,000	252,250[a]
Kuwait	10,000	500	1,900	12,400
Oman	11,500	1,000	2,000	14,500
Qatar	9,000	400	300	9,700
Saudi Arabia	35,000	2,200	14,500	51,700[b]
United Arab Emirates	40,000	1,000	1,500	42,500

[a]Includes conscripts (Iran: 100,000; Iraq: 195,000).
[b]Excludes the National Guard (30,000).
Source: The Military Balance 1981-1982 (London: International Institute for Strategic Studies, 1981), pp. 49-51, 53, 55-56, 58.

TABLE 6.8

Combat Aircraft and Tanks in Persian Gulf States

Country	Combat Aircraft		Tanks	
	1981-82	On Order	1981-82	On Order
Bahrain	—	—	—	—
Iran	100[a]	—	1,630	—
Iraq	335[a]	174 (MIG & Mirage)	2,600[b]	T-62 & AMX-30
Kuwait	50	—	240	Scorpion
Oman	38	12 (Jaguar)	18	—
Qatar	9	14 (Mirage & Alpha jet)	24	—
Saudi Arabia	139	47 (F-15)	630	170 (AMX-30)
United Arab Emirates	51	—	135	25 (mostly Scorpion)

[a]Losses make estimates only tentative.
[b]Some captured Iranian tanks may have been taken into service.
Source: The Military Balance 1981-82 (London: International Institute for Strategic Studies, 1981), pp. 49-51, 53, 55-56, 58.

CHALLENGES AND PROSPECTS:
THE PERSISTENT TRIANGLE

Throughout this volume, the record has clearly indicated that U.S. policy makers as well as gulf leaders are convinced that United States-Persian Gulf relations cannot be viewed in isolation from the Arab-Israeli (or Palestinian) conflict or from the United States' support for Israel. Since the late 1940s, some U.S. officials have always warned the government of this triangular relationship; the October 1973 War again pushed this relationship into the forefront of regional politics. Nor is this the view of Arab leaders only; gulf businessmen and intellectuals have openly recognized this United States-Persian Gulf-Palestine linkage and have urged their governments to conduct their foreign policies with this in mind. The data presented in this book also indicate that gulf elite representatives have even urged the leaders of the recently formed Gulf Cooperation Council to push for a resolution of the Palestinian conflict.

Since the early 1970s, every U.S. president and every gulf leader have linked United States' interests in the region to the need for a resolution of the Arab-Israeli conflict. During a meeting in Riyadh in February 1980, former National Security Advisor Zbigniew Brzezinski told Prince Fahd that the "United States will remain committed to obtaining a peaceful accommodation between the Arabs and the Israelis, with particular recognition of the importance of making progress on the Palestinian issue."[24] On August 8, 1981, Prince Fahd announced his eight-point peace plan, stating that a real linkage exists between gulf security and a resolution of the Palestinian conflict. Saudi and other Arab leaders have frequently stated that regional security can only be enhanced through a settlement granting the right of self-determination to the Palestinians and the right of existence to all states in the region, including Israel.

The triangle has persisted, and it would be the height of naiveté to believe that U.S. interests in the gulf would ever be secure without a Palestinian homeland. This position cannot be argued away by the logic of a Soviet threat, no matter how real, nor can it be wished away by Israeli occupation, no matter how stubborn. It has been argued that resolving the conflict would not eliminate other elements of instability in the gulf. This is true, but the conflict heads the list. It has also been stated, particularly by U.S. government officials, that the Saudis and other gulf peoples do not really like the Palestinians, and ipso facto their statements linking the conflict to the gulf are only for public consumption. This is partly true, but what this argument ignores is the fact that the Saudi leadership now believes that resolving the conflict is in Saudi Arabia's best national interest, regardless of the Saudis' "brotherly love" for the Palestinians.

The Saudis believe that by granting the Palestinians a homeland, a major cause of psychopolitical frustration would disappear, and if the United States would champion such a move, then the U.S.-Saudi "special relationship" would prosper.

The persistent triangle presents U.S. foreign policy makers with a very serious challenge, which Washington cannot long ignore without jeopardizing its interests in the gulf. This is not to say that United States' economic interests would begin to suffer precipitously, but it does mean that continued close identification with the United States in the absence of a settlement would become a source of embarrassment to the Saudi leadership. Some younger princes within the royal family are already questioning the efficacy of the U.S. connection. Again, the basic question is: What will happen to this "special relationship" if the present Saudi regime is replaced by a more nationalistically conscious leadership?

The United States faces other major challenges in the Persian Gulf that are not related to the Palestinian conflict. The most important challenge is the reestablishment of relations with Iran and Iraq, two of the gulf's three significant states. It is unrealistic to discuss any form of regional strategic consensus arrangement in the Persian Gulf/Arabian Peninsula region involving the United States without the participation of Iran and Iraq. Other challenges include supporting gulf states in their efforts to "open up" their regimes to some form of popular participation and to initiate gradual developmental programs. Of course, undergirding all of these challenges is the need to maintain an ongoing dialogue between the United States and the Persian Gulf governments.

The Iraq-Iran war and internal destabilizing plots in some gulf countries are a reminder that the flow of gulf oil might be interrupted because of factors other than direct Soviet aggression. If any kind of protracted conflict similar to the Iraq-Iran war should hit Saudi Arabia or if a major internecine or communal violence should break out in the eastern province of Saudi Arabia, an interruption in the flow of oil would be highly probable. Such a development would have a catastrophic effect on the economies of the industrial world. Consider the following testimony before the Senate Energy Committee on April 19, 1980:

> [A] nine million barrel per day cutback in Persian Gulf exports [about equivalent to the loss of Saudi Arabian production] for one year—assuming that competitive bidding for remaining oil supplies occurs—would cause an estimated 7 percent decrease in the U.S. gross national product, a 9 percent decrease in Western Europe, and a 10 percent decrease in Japan. For the loss of all

supplies from the Gulf for a year, about 18 million barrels per day, the estimated losses are 18 percent of the U.S. GNP, 23 percent for Europe, and 27 percent for Japan. In this latter case, the loss [in 1980 dollars] to the U.S. would be about $520 billion if the cut were to take place in 1982; for the OECD countries in total, it would be about $1,500 billion.[25]

The United States' and Persian Gulf governments have forged a functional system of partnerships—economic and strategic. As the author indicated elsewhere, for this partnership to survive, "it must be creative, multidimensional, mutually beneficial, and open, that is, subject to scrutiny."[26] This partnership, which started in the mid-1970s, is entering a new stage of relations. The United States is more concerned with Soviet expansion and whether such expansion would "engulf the Gulf" but the gulf states are more assertive in this decade than they were in the previous one.

The indigenous populations are more educated than ever and more than ever aware of the issues that are of concern to their countries. When the United States and Bahrain signed the Jufair agreement in December to provide COMIDEASTFOR homeporting facilities in Bahrain, there was barely a dissenting voice in the gulf. Today, ten years later, it is evident that gulf countries, governments and elites alike, are clear in their opposition to foreign military presence in the area.

The gulf Arab states also face several major challenges that they cannot ignore if they hope to become influential actors in regional and international politics.

The most significant challenge is to present a clear, negotiable, and unified program of action for a resolution of the Palestinian conflict. The Saudi peace plan announced by Prince Fahd in August 1981 was a commendable step toward peace. However, with the derailment of that plan at the Arab summit at Fez in November 1981, the need of a unified position on this issue is more urgent than ever. Until the Arab states can manage their own affairs properly, no outside power can or will provide them with a solution to their problems or an easy remedy to their frustrations regarding Israel. Unlike most formerly colonized areas, the Arab world, of which the gulf is a part, has succeeded in throwing off the old colonial rule only to be psychologically and physically dominated by Israel. It is unrealistic to think that the outside world can come to the rescue as long as the Arab world does nothing. To quote a recent newspaper column in a related context: "As long as they leave their future up to others—Israelis, fellow Arabs, Americans or whoever—they will have no future."[27]

A second major challenge facing the Persian Gulf is an educational one directly related to U.S. foreign policy. If Arab states desire to influence U.S. foreign policy, they must first learn about the making of U.S. foreign policy in Washington. Policy decisions are made by a government in which interest groups and their lobbyists constantly attempt to influence the making of policy. In the last three decades, some of the most prominent lobbying efforts have been on behalf of Israel, Eastern Europe, Taiwan, and Greece. No Arab lobby of substance has ever existed for any significant period of time. The Saudi lobbying efforts on behalf of the F-15 in the spring of 1978 and the AWACS in the fall of 1981 were highly successful but limited to specific cases.

On the whole, Arab lobbying in Washington has yet to reach a sophisticated level and has yet to convey an image of effectiveness and respectability. Lobbying and public relations have become an art requiring funding, staffing, planning, expertise, analysis, and above all a functioning system for the gathering and dissemination of information. To become a reputable source of the data on which congressmen and their staff depend for information, any lobbying effort must be rational, clear, calm, diligent, consistent, and committed.

Another challenge facing the gulf Arab states is to present a coherent policy approach toward the United States with the twin objective of: accepting the Arab position as being in line with U.S. national interest; and exerting effective influence on Israel to participate genuinely in the peace process. The first part of this position would include programs regarding questions of security and stability in the gulf. The contradiction of U.S. "protection" without U.S. "presence" will have to be resolved by the gulf states, not by the United States.

A final challenge facing Persian Gulf governments is internal in nature. It pertains to the establishment of a functional system of partnership between the rulers and the ruled in which the people would be invited to participate in the governing of their countries. In the final analysis, regional security and stability are directly linked to internal stability, which in turn can be served through an effective system of popular political participation in government. Until Arabs become true citizens in their own country, internal political stability will always be problematic.

Finally, this book has attempted to present the view from within the gulf and to relate this view to questions of regional stability and security and to the gulf's ability to assess correctly the interests and concerns of outside powers in gulf developments. It is this "view from within" that U.S. policy makers must recognize and accommodate if the 1980s are expected to pass without a major confrontation.

NOTES

1. Herschel Kanter, "U.S. Military Options in the Persian Gulf and Indian Ocean: Why We Were Not Prepared." Paper presented at the American Political Science Association's annual meeting in New York City, September 3-6, 1981, p. 12. Unpublished.

2. Ibid. The distances are 7,000 miles by air, 8,000 miles through the Suez Canal, and 12,000 miles around South Africa.

3. Ibid., p. 13.

4. Harold Brown, U.S. Security Policy in Southwest Asia: A Case Study in Complexity (Washington, D.C.: School of Advanced International Studies, 1981), pp. 2-3.

5. Ibid., p. 4.

6. Ibid., p. 5.

7. Ibid.

8. Ibid.

9. David B. Ottoway, "Oman Expects U.S. Help for Use of Its Bases," Washington Post, April 7, 1982, pp. A1, A17.

10. Brown, Security Policy in Southwest Asia, p. 4.

11. The Oil Import Question: A Report on the Relationship of Oil Imports to the National Security (Washington, D.C.: U.S. Government Printing Office, February 1970), p. 31.

12. Sam H. Schurr, Energy Research Needs (Washington, D.C.: Resources for the Future, October 1971), p. X-89.

13. Ibid., p. X-71.

14. Lester A. Sobel, ed., Energy Crisis, Vol. 1 1969-1973 (New York: Facts on File, 1973), pp. 8, 18-19, 29, 41-42, 53, 78, 107-8, 176, 199.

15. Project Independence (Washington, D.C.: Federal Energy Administration, November 1974).

16. Ibid., Introduction.

17. Ibid., p. 407.

18. Ibid., p. 405.

19. Ibid.

20. U.S. Interests in, and Policies Toward, the Persian Gulf, 1980. Hearings before the Subcommittee on Europe and the Middle East of the Committee on Foreign Affairs, House of Representatives, 96th Cong., 2nd sess. (Washington, D.C.: U.S. Government Printing Office, 1980), p. 461.

21. U.S. Security Interests in the Persian Gulf. Report of a Staff Study Mission to the Persian Gulf, Middle East, and Horn of Africa, October 21-November 13, 1980, to the Committee on Foreign Affairs, House of Representatives (Washington, D.C.: U.S. Government Printing Office, 1981), pp. 20, 27, 32, 53, 60.

22. Saudi Arabia and the United States: The New Context in an Evolving "Special Relationship." Report prepared for the Subcommittee on Europe and the Middle East of the Committee on Foreign Affairs, House of Representatives (Washington, D.C.: U.S. Government Printing Office, 1981), pp. 48–51.

23. Ibid., p. 42.

24. Ibid., p. 59.

25. Security Interests in the Persian Gulf, p. 84.

26. Emile A. Nakhleh, Arab-American Relations in the Persian Gulf (Washington, D.C.: American Enterprise Institute, 1975), p. 70.

27. Stephen S. Rosenfeld, "Are the Palestinians Serious?" Washington Post, April 9, 1982, p. A19.

BIBLIOGRAPHY

BOOKS

Abir, Mordechai. Oil, Power and Politics: Conflict in Arabia, the Red Sea and the Gulf. London: Frank Cass, 1974.

Albaharna, Husain M. The Legal Status of the Arabian Gulf States. Manchester, England: Manchester University Press, 1968.

Ali, Sheikh Rustum. Saudi Arabia and Oil Diplomacy. New York: Praeger, 1976.

Al-Otaiba, Mana Saeed. OPEC and the Petroleum Industry. New York: John Wiley, 1975.

American Foreign Policy Institute. The Impact of the Iranian Events Upon Persian Gulf and United States Security. Washington, D.C., 1979.

Annual Report, 1980. Riyadh, Saudi Arabia: Saudi Arabian Monetary Agency, 1980.

Anthony, John Duke. Arab States of Lower Gulf. Washington, D.C.: Middle East Institute, 1975.

The Arab Oil-Producing States of the Gulf: Political and Economic Developments. Washington, D.C.: American Enterprise Institute, 1980). Special double issue of AEI Foreign Policy and Defense Review.

The Atlantic Council. Oil and Turmoil: Western Policies in the Middle East. Washington, D.C., September 1979.

_____. After Afghanistan—The Long Haul. Washington, D.C., March 1980.

Bill, James A., and Carl Leiden. Politics in the Middle East. Boston: Little, Brown, 1979.

Burrell, R. M. The Persian Gulf. New York: Library Press, 1972.

Chubin, Shahram. Soviet Policy toward Iran and the Gulf. Adelphi Papers, no. 157. London: International Institute for Strategic Studies, 1980.

Cottrell, Alvin J., and F. Bray. Military Forces in the Persian Gulf. Washington, D.C.: Center for Strategic and International Studies, 1978.

Dawisha, Adeed. Saudi Arabia's Search for Security. Adelphi Papers, no. 158. London: International Institute for Strategic Studies, 1979.

Dessouki, Ali E. H. The Iraq-Iran War: Issues of Conflict and Prospects for Settlement. Princeton, N.J.: Princeton University, Center of International Studies, 1981.

Duignan, Peter, and L. H. Gann. The Middle East and North Africa: The Challenge to Western Security. Stanford: Hoover Institution Press, 1981.

Eden, David G. Oil and Development in the Middle East. New York: Praeger, 1979.

Graham, Robert. Iran: The Illusion of Power. London: Groom Helm, 1978.

Halliday, Fred. Arabia Without Sultans. New York: Vintage, 1974.

_____. Mercenaries: "Counter-Insurgency" in the Gulf. Nottingham, England: Russell Press, 1977.

_____. After the Shah. Washington, D.C.: Institute for Policy Studies, 1979.

_____. Iran: Dictatorship and Development. Middlesix, England: Penguin, 1979.

Hurewitz, J. C., ed. The Middle East and North Africa in World Politics: A Documentary Record. 2nd ed., vol. 1. New Haven: Yale University Press, 1975.

Khadduri, Majid. Republican Iraq: A Study in Iraqi Politics Since the Revolution of 1958. London: Oxford University Press, 1969.

_____. Socialist Iraq: A Study in the Iraqi Politics Since 1968. Washington, D.C.: Middle East Institute, 1978.

Kissinger, Henry. White House Years. Boston: Little, Brown, 1979.

Knanerhase, Ramon. The Saudi Arabian Economy. New York: Praeger, 1975.

Kolko, Gabriel, and Joyce Kolko. The Limits of Power: The World and United States Foreign Policy, 1945-54. New York: Harper & Row, 1972.

Koury, Enver M. Oil and Geopolitics in the Persian Gulf Area: A Center of Power. Beirut, Lebanon: Catholic Press, 1973.

_____. The United Arab Emirates: Its Political System and Politics. Hyattsville, Md.: Institute of Middle Eastern and North African Affairs, 1980.

Koury, Enver M., and E. A. Nakhleh. The Arabian Peninsula, Red Sea, and Gulf: Strategic Considerations. Hyattsville, Md.: Institute of Middle Eastern and North African Affairs, 1979.

Long, David E. The Persian Gulf: An Introduction to Its People, Politics, and Economics. Boulder, Colo.: Westview Press, 1976.

MacDonald, Charles. Iran, Saudi Arabia, and the Law of the Sea: Political Interaction and Legal Development in the Persian Gulf. Westport, Conn.: Greenwood Press, 1980.

McLaurin, R. D., ed. The Political Role of Minority Groups in the Middle East. New York: Praeger, 1979.

The Middle East Institute. The Gulf and the Peninsula: American Interests and Policies in the 'Eighties. Washington, D.C.: 34th Annual Conference, September 1980.

Nakhleh, Emile A. Arab-American Relations in the Persian Gulf. Washington, D.C.: American Enterprise Institute, 1975.

_____. The United States and Saudi Arabia: A Policy Analysis. Washington, D.C.: American Enterprise Institute, 1975.

_____. Bahrain: Political Development in a Modernizing Society. Lexington, Mass.: Lexington, 1976.

Niblock, Tim, ed. Social and Economic Development in the Arab Gulf. London: Groom Helm, 1980.

Noyes, James H. The Clouded Lens: Persian Gulf Security and U.S. Policy. Stanford: Hoover Institution Press, 1979.

Odell, Peter R. Oil and World Power. 5th ed. New York: Penguin, 1979.

Quandt, William B. Decade of Decision: American Policy toward the Arab-Israeli Conflict, 1967-1976. Indianapolis: Bobbs-Merrill, 1977.

_____. Saudi Arabia in the 1980s: Foreign Policy, Security, and Oil. Washington, D.C.: Brookings Institution, 1981.

Ricks, Thomas. The Iranian People's Revolution: Its Nature and Implications for the Gulf States. Washington, D.C.: Georgetown University, Center for Contemporary Arab Studies, 1979.

Rubin, Barry. Paved with Good Intentions: The American Experience and Iran. London and New York: Oxford University Press, 1980.

Sampson, Anthony. The Arms Bazaar: From Lebanon to Lockheed. New York: Bantam, 1978.

Sivard, Ruth Leger. World Military and Social Expenditures, 1981. Leesburg, Va.: World Priorities, 1981.

Statistical Summary, 1981. Riyadh, Saudi Arabia: Saudi Arabian Monetary Agency, 1981.

Stempel, John D. Inside the Iranian Revolution. Bloomington: Indiana University Press, 1981.

Stork, Joe. Middle East Oil and the Energy Crisis. New York: Monthly Review Press, 1975.

Tahtinen, Dale R. Arms in the Indian Ocean: Interests and Challenges. Washington, D.C.: American Enterprise Institute, 1977.

_____. National Security Challenges to Saudi Arabia. Washington, D.C.: American Enterprise Institute, 1978.

Yodfat, A., and M. Abir. In the Direction of the Persian Gulf: The Soviet Union and the Persian Gulf. London: Frank Cass, 1977.

Yorke, Valerie. The Gulf in the 1980s. London: Royal Institute of International Affairs, 1980.

ARTICLES

Chubin, Shahram. "Regional Perceptions of the Impact of Soviet Policy in the Middle East." Paper presented at the Woodrow Wilson Center, Washington, D.C. (September 1981). Unpublished.

Collins, John M., et al. "Petroleum Imports from the Persian Gulf: Use of U.S. Armed Force to Ensure Supplies." Washington, D.C.: Congressional Research Service, February 1980. Unpublished.

Remnek, Richard B. "Superpower Security Interests in the Indian Ocean Area." Washington, D.C., June 1980. Unpublished.

Ross, Dennis. "Considering Soviet Threats to the Persian Gulf." Paper presented at the Woodrow Wilson·Center, Washington, D.C. (September 1981). Unpublished.

Tucker, Robert W. "American Power and the Persian Gulf." Commentary 70 (November 1980):25-41.

Van Hollen, Christopher. "Don't Engulf the Gulf." Foreign Affairs 59 (Summer 1981):1064-78.

Zartman, I. William. "The Power of American Purposes." The Middle East Journal 35 (Spring 1981):163-77.

INDEX

ABOUT THE AUTHOR

EMILE A. NAKHLEH is professor of political science and chairman of the Department of History and Political Science at Mount Saint Mary's College, Emmitsburg, Maryland. He is also an adjunct scholar at the American Enterprise Institute, Washington, D.C. Professor Nakhleh was a Fulbright senior fellow (Bahrain, 1972-73), a National Endowment for the Humanities research fellow with residency at the American Enterprise Institute (Washington, 1979-80), and a Woodrow Wilson guest scholar (Washington, summer 1979). Dr. Nakhleh has traveled extensively in the Middle East, has lectured widely both in the United States and overseas, and has written and contributed to numerous books and journals. His most recent books include: A Palestinian Agenda for the West Bank and Gaza (1980); The West Bank and Gaza: Toward the Making of a Palestinian State (1979); Bahrain: Political Development in a Modernizing Society (1976); The United States and Saudi Arabia: A Policy Analysis (1975); and Arab-American Relations in the Persian Gulf (1975).